AN ACTION GUIDE TO
SCHOOL
IMPROVEMENT

Susan Loucks-Horsley and Leslie F. Hergert

ASCD/The NETWORK

About the Authors

SUSAN LOUCKS-HORSLEY is the Director of Research and Development at The NETWORK, Inc. in Andover, Massachusetts, where she oversees projects studying various aspects of the school improvement process, examining the effects of different forms of assistance and support, and developing materials and models for improving schools and classrooms. She began her work in the school improvement area with nine years at the Texas Research and Development Center for Teacher Education, where she helped develop the Concerns-Based Adoption Model and explored the change process. Her three years at The NETWORK have included contributions to a three-year nationwide study of federally supported school improvement strategies, culminating in a ten-volume report, *People, Policies, and Practices: Examining the Chain of School Improvement*.

LESLIE F. HERGERT is the Director of School Services at The NETWORK, Inc. She oversees technical assistance and training projects to assist in school improvement. In the ten years she has been at The NETWORK, she has helped schools find and use research-based resources, provided management and leadership training for administrators, and led school improvement teams engaged in long-term improvement efforts. For the past five years, she has focused on educational equity for women, developing model programs for school district use. She is completing development of a simulation board game called *Making Change for School Improvement*.

Price: $5.00
ASCD Stock Number: 611-85360
ISBN: 0-87120-130-5
Library of Congress
  Card Catalog Number: 85-070038

March 1985

Contents

Foreword

High on almost everyone's agenda these days is improving
schools. Governors, corporation executives, and ordinary
citizens are determined that education must change. Some
of us contend that schools are more successful than the public seems
to think, but we too want them to be even better.

There is much less agreement, however, about the kinds of
changes that are needed—and about how those changes should be
made. Much has already been written about what schools should
do: stiffen graduation requirements, improve reading
comprehension, ensure equal opportunity, teach thinking skills. . . .

Some of those who advocate these changes have suggestions for
how to bring them about, but most have little to say on that subject.
Often they assume it's just a matter of convincing reluctant
educators to try something new or of some authority issuing the
necessary directives.

Susan Loucks-Horsley and Leslie Hergert know it is not that
simple, but they also have plenty of evidence that improvement
programs can succeed. They outline a seven-step process and offer
specific practical suggestions for what to do at each step. They speak
directly to anyone who proposes to undertake an improvement
effort, then pause occasionally to reflect on ramifications of their
advice.

Action-minded administrators and consultants will treasure this *Guide*, not only because of the clarity of its language and ideas, but because it is grounded in practice. The authors have counseled and observed hundreds of schools involved in a variety of improvement projects. From their rich personal experience and their informed analysis of research, some of which they conducted, they have distilled this useful volume. May we use it well.

PHIL C. ROBINSON
ASCD President, 1984–85

Introduction

You are about to embark on a school improvement effort. You may have been assigned by the superintendent to lead a school effectiveness project for your district. You may be part of your school's committee to develop a new discipline policy, a new science curriculum, or a computer lab. Or you may have decided, on your own, to try to get your school to include women and minorities in its social studies curriculum.

As you consider your next steps, don't be fooled. School improvement is a difficult task, but it is not an impossible one. For years, researchers reported mostly "doom and gloom," claiming that local educators were too unsophisticated and were too mired in daily problems to really change their schools. Yet, those same educators have developed new and better ways to teach reading, writing, and math skills while responding to desegregation orders and making room for mainstreamed handicapped children.

Fortunately for others who have not yet followed suit, research has begun to document successful school improvement efforts and the effective schools that result. We are beginning to understand much more about the complexities of schools and what factors contribute to their improvement.

Over the past ten years, we have been involved with hundreds of schools, helping them to serve their students better and observing their efforts to improve. Our research and service activities have taken us into schools on Indian reservations, in sprawling bedroom communities, in inner cities, in tiny seacoast towns, and deep into the Florida Everglades. We wrote this book to share the principles and strategies we have used and observed in a wide variety of school improvement efforts.[1]

What do we mean by "school improvement"? We use this term quite broadly to include the pursuit of any goal that benefits students and that has as its focus the classroom and school building. These goals may include, as have our own experiences, the following:

● Changing an elementary school's reading program in response to low achievement scores.

● Developing and implementing a districtwide science curriculum for elementary grades.

● Implementing Edmond's "correlates of effective schools" in high schools.

● Applying advances in technology to a district's special education program.

● Increasing equitable treatment and opportunities for all students in a large urban school district.

A large number of these efforts focus on curriculum and instruction, but some target more elusive areas such as discipline, school climate, and instructional leadership. Some begin at the district level or above (for example, in response to a state or federal regulation); others are initiated by someone in an individual school. Some are voluntary; some are mandatory.

Regardless of their content, impetus, or point of initiation, we have observed direct outcomes in successful programs—increased reading achievement, ongoing use of new curriculum materials, and community involvement. At the same time, we have observed schools expanding their capacity to solve their own organizational problems by initiating and supporting necessary changes.

Solving persistent problems and increasing the capacity to attack future ones is what school improvement is all about. In this book we try to reflect on our experiences and synthesize them into a

---

[1]We provide a variety of references throughout this book. However, major ones that report our own research and experiences at The NETWORK and at the University of Texas's Research and Development Center for Teacher Education are: Crandall and associates, 1982; Ford and Hergert, 1979; Loucks and associates, 1983; Loucks and Hall, 1979; and Louis and Rosenblum, 1981.

set of concrete steps and activities. We share strategies and tools that can be useful along the way.

We think you will find this book different from others currently available, in part because we have formed some beliefs that appear to contradict the "conventional wisdom" about improving schools. Some people, in fact, find these beliefs fairly outrageous. Here are just a few:

1. *Acting* is better than *planning.* Protracted needs assessment can be worse than none at all.

2. The principal is not *the* key to school improvement. Although the principal is important, so are many other people. The principal alone is seldom able to ensure the success of a school improvement effort, and principals can even be worked around.

3. Thinking you can truly create ownership at the beginning of a project is ridiculous. Like trust, ownership and commitment build and develop over time through the actual work of improving a school.

4. Help and support given teachers *after* planning and initial training is much more crucial for success than the best training money can buy.

5. Coercion is not always bad. A firm push, coupled with lots of help, can launch a project on a path to success.

6. New programs and practices imported from somewhere else offer a viable, cost-effective—and in most cases, preferable— alternative to major development efforts.

Having made these rash statements and defying many experts, we must add that all activities that involve planning and supporting school improvement must be based on a combination of these premises and others we discuss later. Neither mandates, back-end support, nor quick action can stand alone and lead to success. Each situation calls for its own combination that is sensitive to the needs, experiences, and inclinations of the people involved. Such is the "art" of school improvement. We have tried to provide ideas and techniques, but, like a good cook, you will have to identify the ingredients at hand and combine them using your own style to make a satisfying and nourishing meal.

Who Is This Book For?

One of our beliefs is that it takes the energy of a lot of people, over a fairly long time, to improve a school. Therefore, we offer this book to anyone with the commitment or in a position to be involved. Primarily, we have written it for educators responsible for an improvement effort in their own community: for the principal engaged in school reform, for the district technology coordinator, for the teachers on the Human Rights Committee, for the department head trying to change the emphasis of the department, and for the administrator responsible for the new staff evaluation process. Some of these people have authority, others don't. We have tended to assume less authority rather than more, because ordering that something be done so seldom works!

Secondarily, we think the contents of this book have important implications for those who train teachers and administrators (for example, in colleges and universities), for those who provide expertise and support to schools from the outside (for example, consultants, intermediate agencies), and for those who make decisions that schools have to implement (for example, local school boards, state and federal education agencies, and legislators). Schooling and its improvement is everybody's business. It is critical that those who are involved both directly and indirectly know how to make things happen.

A Model for Viewing the Improvement Process

Before launching into the substance of the book, we describe a practical, research-based conceptual framework to explain, in part, why we believe and suggest the things we do. Because the process of school improvement requires change, we find it helpful to apply a model of the change process to schools' efforts to improve. The Concerns-Based Adoption Model (CBAM) (Loucks and Hall, 1979) describes the changing feelings of individuals (teachers and administrators) as they learn about, prepare for, use, and refine new practices. Initially, people have self-oriented concerns: What is the new practice? How will it affect me? When these concerns are resolved, concerns about managing the new practice dominate: How do I do it? How can I keep it from taking so much time? When will I be able to anticipate all the surprises that seem to occur every day? Finally, when the management tasks are mastered, concerns turn to the impact of the practice on students: Are they learning? What can I do better? The CBAM defines seven stages of concern. As illustrated in Figure 1, they generally flow from a focus on self, to task, to impact (Hall and Loucks, 1978).

What does this sequence of concerns mean for school improvement? First, research has shown that plans designed to

Figure 1.
Stages of Concern: Typical Expressions of Concern
About the Innovation

Stages of Concern	Expressions of Concern
6 Refocusing	I have some ideas about something that would work even better.
5 Collaboration	I am concerned about relating what I am doing with what other instructors are doing.
4 Consequence	How is my use affecting kids?
3 Management	I seem to be spending all my time in getting material ready.
2 Personal	How will using it affect me?
1 Informational	I would like to know more about it.
0 Awareness	I am not concerned about it (the innovation).

From G.E. Hall and S.F. Loucks, "Teacher Concerns as a Basis for Facilitating Staff Development," *Teachers College Record* 80, 1 (1978): 36–53.

address people's concerns as they emerge heighten the potential for success. This includes the ways people are involved in decision making, the training and follow-up help they receive, the expectations set and voiced by people with "clout," the assignment of support roles, and the project's timeline. As we proceed through the book, we describe how concerns theory affects decisions in each of these areas.

The most important reason we rely so heavily on the notion of concerns is that it keeps us closely in touch with the real key to improvement—people. Teachers, administrators, parents, and students all have contributions to make, and these contributions can be optimized if we organize a school improvement effort with their concerns uppermost in our minds.

A Guide to the Book

We have divided the book into seven linear steps. The steps, depicted as they relate to the school improvement process in Figure 2, are:

Step 1—Establishing the School Improvement Project
Step 2—Assessment and Goal Setting
Step 3—Identifying an Ideal Solution
Step 4—Preparing for Implementation
Step 5—Implementing

Step 6—Review
Step 7—Maintenance and Institutionalization

Figure 2.
Our School As We'd Like It To Be

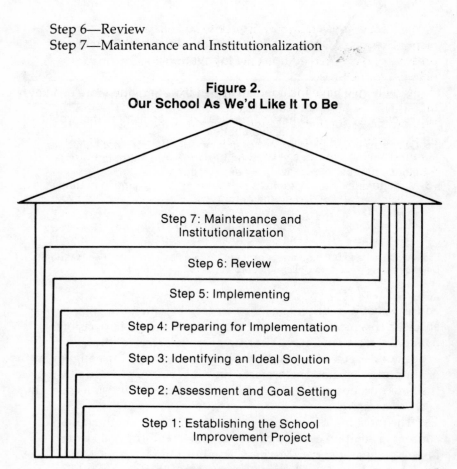

Step 7: Maintenance and
Institutionalization

Step 6: Review

Step 5: Implementing

Step 4: Preparing for Implementation

Step 3: Identifying an Ideal Solution

Step 2: Assessment and Goal Setting

Step 1: Establishing the School
Improvement Project

Our School As It Is Now

Seven steps seem manageable and a linear process imposes some order on a complex situation. However, if you pick up the book in the middle of your project, you may find that you have already done some of the early steps instinctively. And even if you start at the beginning, you may find yourself working on two steps at once. Be flexible and thoughtful about meeting the needs of your own situation.

For each of the steps, we explain what is involved and why, and provide tools and procedures to select from. At the end of each step we include a "dialogue" between the two authors—one who has spent years studying school improvement, the other facilitating it. We discuss ideas that may appear to be contradictory and respond to questions that constantly come up when the ideas are presented to a variety of audiences. We hope these dialogues add richness to the process.

Finally, we have included an appendix to provide more of a key ingredient—school improvement resources available to schools. Without knowing the full range of resources available, efforts to improve can be long and hard. Although we all like to put our own stamp on what we do, the world simply does not need another wheel.

Susan Loucks-Horsley and Leslie F. Hergert

Step 1: Establishing the School Improvement Project

I t's time to begin. Your school improvement project may have emerged from a district or school priority, or it may be your own initiative. It may focus on a particular content area, or it may be totally unfocused at the onset. You may be beginning with a raft of supporters, or you may be launching the effort on your own. Whichever description fits, the way you begin is important.

The effort you are undertaking will need to be made a "legitimate" district or school activity. Even if you are taking on the task informally, it will help to think of it as a project. In this section, we describe preliminary tasks necessary to establish the project:

- Clarify your charge
- Negotiate for resources
- Build a base of relationships
- Consider using an outside consultant
- Form a school improvement team.

Clarify Your Charge

Think first about what kinds of outcomes would be acceptable to you and the role you want to play in reaching those outcomes. Then negotiate with the appropriate administrator. You may decide that you want your school improvement project to operate in three schools, with you serving as the on-site facilitator. The superintendent may believe that the project should function in every school in the district and that your role should be that of a planner and resource identifier. The two notions are each acceptable, but they are incompatible. Don't assume that everyone understands the job as you do—find out what the assumptions are and negotiate until you get a role you can accept.

Negotiate for Resources

Resources can mean money, time, or services. Find out what you can get. Money may be budgeted for a committee or project, or it may be available for substitute teachers or for travel. Time may be allocated to release you to work on this effort, for teachers to be released from classes, or for a designated administrator to meet regularly with you to serve as a sounding board. Services may mean that a secretary is assigned to perform clerical tasks for you or that an outside agency can provide assistance. A good rule of thumb is, "If you don't ask, you don't get." So ask.

Remember that this is just your first round of looking for resources. Later you will be asking for resources to support the implementation effort, a much larger and more important set of resources. This initial negotiation is for resources to support the planning and management of the effort. You will learn something about how much of a priority your job is, where some of the restraints are, and so forth. Figure 3 lists some of the resources you might get for your project.

Build a Base of Relationships

As you negotiate, you will realize that you are also trying to make friends and allies for your project. You will want both "top level" and "grass roots" support. You will meet first with the administrator above you who is overseeing the project. There may also be other administrators with an interest in the project whose support you want to obtain. If you are an administrator, you may know more about how the project came to be than if you are a teacher or someone hired for the job. In either case, you are in a relatively new situation and set of relationships. You may want to know what others hope will come out of the project, either generally or specifically. You may find that someone is responding to outside pressure—a parent group, for example. You may find that your

Figure 3.
Possible Resources

Money
—A budget for the committee to use at its discretion
—Substitute teachers
—Materials
—Travel
—Conference fees
—Stipends for extra time
—Consultant work funds

Time (which, sometimes, is money)
—Release time for teachers
—For attending conferences, visiting programs . . .
—For inservice
—For staff and board meetings
—Agreement to eliminate part of your job to take on this task
—Administrative support
—For other committee work

Services
—Secretarial help (typing minutes and letters, photocopying)
—Consultant or outside help (hired or free from a funded agency)
—Help from volunteers, parents, students

project is a "mission" for someone. You may also find that one or more administrator feels threatened by the project or by your having responsibility for it. It is important to know what and whose purposes the project is serving and could serve. In these first meetings, you will be trying to describe your initial vision of the project in ways that others can "buy into." You also want to find out what is important to *them*. Sometimes, other ideas and purposes can be incorporated; sometimes not. You also need to know which administrators are responsible for what and who has access to which resources.

In one school selected to participate in a federally funded project, the linking agent (one of the authors) thought her first meeting with the faculty would be an easy one—the focus was reading (not a controversial topic), and the project was well funded (so the school would get training and funds it would not normally get). She was astonished at the hostility of the teachers *and* the principal, who proceeded to "forget" his next two meetings with her. It was only when she confronted him directly that she learned that everyone in the school thought their school had been singled out as the worst one in the district. She convinced the principal that her job was to help the school and that they would work together to change that image. He became an ardent supporter of the project and a true instructional leader.

You will want to build a base of support not only among administrators but among teachers and others who will be involved in implementing the changes that will be initiated. How you do this will differ depending on your position in the district or school. In any case, it is usually a good idea to meet with the head of the local teachers' association and to talk informally with people who represent various opinions and role groups. In addition to getting a sense of people's initial reactions to the project ("This is a really exciting idea!" or "Just one more idea dumped on us by the central office."), you will learn more about the people in the district—who has expertise in the area, whose opinion is trusted by others, who is articulate and thoughtful about this topic or about past change efforts.

All of these initial meetings may seem time consuming and even unnecessary in some cases. They are also preliminary to the process itself and may seem to contradict our earlier rule that doing is better than planning. Nevertheless, we strongly recommend that you make the time for these conversations. Each one may be as short as 15 minutes; often they will be informal. They should not drag on for a month. But you will be accomplishing several very important things. First, you will learn things that will help you manage this change effort; second, you will establish yourself as the person in charge; and third, you will be communicating that you care about the views of others in the district and consider them important to your success.

Consider Using an Outside Consultant

Many school districts use outside consultants frequently; others, rarely. At the risk of sounding self-serving (the authors are, in fact, outside consultants), we want to address briefly the value and uses of an outside consultant to oversee the process.

School districts reluctant to use outside consultants generally subscribe to one of the following lines of reasoning:

1. Consultants cost too much money to use as ongoing overseers of the process: We'll bring someone in with expertise we don't have or if we hit a snag. Otherwise, we'll manage the process ourselves.

2. Consultants are unnecessary and sometimes dangerous: They have their own ideas of both the process and the solutions, and they will impose those ideas on us. Their ideas of process usually slow us down and sometimes stir up internal troubles. ("I remember back in the 60s. . . .")

As in most resistance, there are elements of truth here. Consultants do cost money and, if they have an ongoing presence in a school improvement effort, the money adds up. And sometimes particular consultants are not particularly helpful!

The value of an outsider has to do with focused attention and with balance of power. An outside consultant will treat the job of planning and facilitating the effort *as a job*. The principal of a school will be busy meeting the everyday demands of the school and may give short shrift to this "extra" effort. The everyday job of the consultant is to manage these kinds of efforts. Thus, if the effort is important to you and nobody has been given the extra time needed to manage the extra effort, consider using a consultant.

An outsider can also be especially important in balancing power groups and neutralizing factions. An outsider, by definition, is not in one of the district's groups, has no alliances, and will not have to "live" with people over the long haul. Outside consultants have the best chance of being, *and* being perceived as, neutral and fair to all parties and perspectives. In addition, they have no power to gain or lose within the school district (they are not, for example, in line for the superintendency). Consider using an outsider when the situation is politically charged or if the district is divided over an issue.

Of course, many school improvement efforts are either small enough or straightforward enough to be managed by an internal "change agent." Some school districts are large enough that a central office person, depending on role and authority, can play an outsider's role in an individual building. Sometimes an outside consultant can be found who is subsidized by a government or by an other-funded project and who will work at little or no cost to the district. Whether you choose to use outsiders or go it alone, we believe this book will point out some pitfalls and suggest some useful approaches.

Form a School Improvement Team

In order to ensure that various perspectives are included and that the school improvement process has a broad base of support, we recommend the establishment of a multiconstituent school improvement team. Research has shown that a strong administrator with access to resources can successfully initiate a school improvement project without involving others in the planning. Nevertheless, we believe the chances of achieving success with minimal disruption are greater when representatives of key groups are involved in the process.

A school improvement team should be relatively small (five to 15 people) and be led either by the district person responsible for the effort or by an outside facilitator. Which groups should be represented will vary from project to project and from district to district. The team should always include both administrators and teachers from the units that will be affected (elementary/secondary, special education/regular education, counselors/media specialists) and should include various groups in the district (new and experienced teachers, various ethnic groups, cliques). Parents, students, and community members are groups to seriously consider involving on the team because they can have valuable and different perspectives on the problem being addressed. The team's expertise should balance the content being addressed and the process skills, such as planning or problem solving. Last, the team should include people who are open-minded, sensitive to the needs of the whole district, and capable of working well together. Figure 4 provides examples of two different school improvement teams.

Figure 4.
Two Examples of School Improvement Teams

Districtwide Special Education Technology Committee:	Schoolwide Reading Curriculum Committee:
Director of Special Education	Principal
Member, district Technology Committee	Building reading specialist
Two regular teachers (elementary and secondary)	District language arts coordinator
Two special education teachers (elementary and secondary)	Four teachers (two from K–3; two from 4–6)
Building principal	
Two parents	Two parents
One specialist (learning disabled or speech)	

The role of the improvement team should be discussed at the first few meetings, and new issues that arise should be clarified with the appropriate administrator.* Someone, probably you, should be the team leader. If the group is charged with making a recommendation, to whom should the recommendation be made? Will the recommendation be likely to be accepted, or scrutinized carefully by various groups? Does the team have the authority to call meetings, distribute materials, or purchase supplies with a specified amount of money? Who must authorize what? It can be discouraging to a team to put time and energy into a decision, only to find it overturned by an administrator. While this occurrence often cannot be avoided, steps can be taken to minimize the likelihood of its happening.

A Conversation Between the Authors

Hergert: *We recommend using a team of people to oversee the school improvement effort. Yet, often a single person—such as a principal or project director—has the authority and responsibility for improvement.*

A principal once said to me that he couldn't use such a team without an outside facilitator because he would not be able to provide leadership and facilitate the group at the same time. He chose to initiate his curriculum reform efforts single-handedly, putting all his energy into leading and supporting his teachers. Another principal, newly appointed with a charge to "shape up the building," felt that it would have been divisive for him to choose a small group to serve as the team, that if he did so, he would be creating an "insider's group."

Is the research conclusive about the need for a team, or about when to use a team and when to go it alone?

Loucks-Horsley: *No, I wouldn't say the research is at all conclusive in this area. We see many instances where team approaches work, as in the R&D Utilization Program, where problem-solving teams assisted by external change agents succeeded in making improvements in both classrooms and schools (Louis and Rosenblum, 1981). On the other hand, our own study of a variety of strategies used by state and federal governments to support improvements in schools found that projects with*

---

*The NETWORK has developed a board game to prepare teams for engaging in the school improvement process and to work together effectively. *Making Change for School Improvement* takes three hours to play and covers many of the points made in this book. Information about ordering will be available in summer 1985 from The NETWORK, Inc.

strong, forceful leaders who worked single-handedly were more likely to succeed (Huberman, 1983).

Hergert: *That variety of possibilities confirms my own experiences. Although I've had much success using the team approach, I remember a principal who strong-armed his staff into making major changes (from departmentalization to self-contained classrooms, with new reading, writing, and math programs!) and only later won them over. I've also seen principals driven out of schools for such actions.*

Loucks-Horsley: *I think this issue just illustrates one of the underpinnings of this book: it takes many ingredients to make school improvement work. Sometimes not having a formal team can be compensated for by having a clearly perceived need, a high-quality curriculum or instructional approach available to meet that need, and a great deal of relevant and ongoing support for teachers to use the new approach. Teams in and of themselves do not guarantee success. What they seem to do is democratize the process, eliminate or alleviate the initial stress and bad feelings that unilateral mandates can raise, and ensure that the different perspectives that make up a school are considered. Frankly, research indicates that a team approach is messy and time-consuming, and it has no greater potential for failure or success than do nonteam approaches.*

Hergert: *Still, my experience says that a team is usually helpful both for making sure that improvement really happens and for the community-building that the team approach fosters.*

Step 2: Assessment and Goal Setting

An early step of any improvement process is assessment. Although we are convinced that too much emphasis and time are spent on assessment, we recognize the importance of knowing where you are at the start. If you want to lose weight, you first find out how much you weigh, what is the recommended weight for your height, and what your real goal is for weight loss (to look good in a bathing suit? to increase your prospects of long life?). We deliberately did not call this stage "needs assessment" because some people believe that starting with strengths is more useful than starting with needs. Nevertheless, most people, and most schools, start their improvement process from a point of dissatisfaction; thus, we will start there as well.

When educators are asked to define their needs, they frequently do so either in general terms ("We need to provide computer education") or in terms of a solution ("We need programs for gifted children"). It is important to define the need more carefully and openly in order to leave room for a wider range of solutions. For example, the needs of gifted children may be met by a number of solutions, ranging from a separate school for the academically talented to individualized instruction in every classroom in the district. Either of these solutions will draw gasps of dismay from many people in the district. Problem definition can be difficult, tedious, and time consuming, but it can lead to wide satisfaction with the resolution of a recognized problem.

Here is where a representative team can be extremely helpful. Teachers on the team may remind you of the difficulties encountered the last time individualized instruction was tried. Parents may point out that separating the gifted children from the other children may result in isolating them from their friends. If you work alone, you are bound to make an assumption that turns out to be false or to ignore a point of view you know nothing about. A team helps identify, clarify, and balance the concerns of many people and groups.

The first step in defining the problem is to collect data about the nature and severity of the problem. Figure 5, on page 11, is an example of what one school did to define their problem. You or your team will determine what types of data you need. To many people, data mean numbers or test scores. But tests are only one source of student achievement data. Other sources are teacher assessments or student performance indicators (for example, writing samples, books read). Information other than student achievement data may also be helpful. The perceptions of teachers, administrators, or the community may be more of a problem than is actual achievement. Behavior or attitude may be the problem.

Once you have determined your information needs, you must decide where to get it. Standardized test results are always available. Sometimes there are reports of prior assessment that emanate from the district office or that come from a statewide process. New information can be gathered for this particular effort, but it is helpful to build on what is available. Deciding where to collect data involves not only deciding what information is available but also which groups are valuable data resources, including teachers, students, parents, community agencies, employers, and state department of education personnel.

Data sources include (a) classroom, school observations; (b) test scores—aptitude, achievement, national, local; (c) surveys of parents, teachers, and students; (d) interviews of the same groups; and (e) documentation of activities. After you identify sources of data, you can develop and carry out an assessment plan. Interviews, surveys, classroom observations, and meetings of representative people are some strategies to consider. A decision will need to be made about who are the best people to gather specific kinds of information. For example, in some schools, classroom observations

Figure 5.
Sample Problem Statement

Kind of Problem
—Curricular—language arts
—Lack of continuity

Who Is Affected
—All students
—Grades 1–6 (with coordination with kindergarten)
—Teachers

How They Are Affected
—Students
  • Repeating skills they have already mastered (poor use of time)
  • Tuning out
  • Punctuation is poor (CAT scores)
  • Not using skills they have "mastered"; transfer is poor (spelling,
    commas correct on test but later used incorrectly in sentences)

—Teachers
  • Frustrated by frequent changes
  • Having difficulty integrating individual skills into a meaningful whole
  • Don't know what materials and skills students have had, will have
  • Assessment device requires a month to process; teachers don't
    know which specific skills to teach the first month

Evidence
—Teacher observation
—School's scores (CAT) are lower than other schools in the system in
    reading and language

Causes
—Wide variety of programs being used without any link
—Lack of teacher training in use of programs
—Specialist schedule is imposed on teachers
—Communication between teachers is difficult

Goals for Improvement
—Sequential language arts program (integrating reading, spelling,
    listening, writing, speaking, handwriting, grammar)
—Recordkeeping system that can track student progress from year to
    year and within a year
—Improved use of language arts skills in other content areas (skill
    transfer)
—Teachers know where to place students first day of school
—Students enter individualized program at their levels of ability
—Provide enrichment activities for above-average students
—Provide parents with more realistic information about children's
    strengths, weaknesses, and progress
—Improve teacher training to ensure best use of programs
—Prepare teachers to better handle individual needs

may best be done by an objective outsider, whereas in other schools, peer teachers who are trusted might elicit the best information. There are no universal rules for deciding who are the best people to collect the data; the decision will depend on the local situation. In addition to what information will be gathered and who will do it, the needs assessment plan should include a time line indicating when each type of information will be collected.

Be careful not to collect too much data—your analysis tasks will be too great—and to collect data in the most unobtrusive and positive way possible.

After information is collected, you and your team must analyze it. You will be checking your initial understanding of the situation with the additional data you have collected. Be prepared to expand (or even change completely) your initial ideas.

Depending on the nature of the problem, you should examine data for differences based on sex, race, and achievement level. Often, when data are only looked at in total, we miss important problems. This was the case for years with math anxiety among females, a situation which went unnoticed as a problem until female participation rate and test scores were examined separately.

Some planning experts (Clark, for example) have begun to argue against needs assessment. They say that it is difficult to ascertain real needs, that plans usually have little relation to identified needs, and that what people are doing is a better indicator of their values than what they are not doing. They suggest developing a shared vision of the future rather than concentrating on detailing needs and goals that will be of little use (Clark and others, 1980).

An alternative starting point to a needs assessment is a "strengths assessment." If you determine where the strengths of the district lie and what accomplishments or values are important to people, you may be able to begin on an upbeat note that will infuse the whole improvement process.

Design for Building a Shared Vision

Regardless of whether you start with needs assessment or strengths assessment, we believe there is one extremely important rule to follow: Don't spend too much time on assessment.

Whatever you assess will change. After all, in many schools, the entire student body changes every four years; the school board can change completely in that period of time. We have heard of needs assessments that have taken two years to collect data, summarize feedback to various groups, clarify and revise, etc., etc., etc. They say they are "getting people on board" or "involving people in the process." We say that's too long and there are better ways to involve people. You run a terrible risk of using up energy before you really get started and of losing the momentum. *When you have a choice between planning and doing, choose doing.*

When the assessment is completed and analyzed, the results should be fed back to people in the district or school. A written report could be developed, or the report could be presented orally. The report should be concise, yet clearly substantiated, and should be easy to understand so it can be shared widely throughout the school community. Various teachers, administrators, and parents should be asked to react to and revise the report so that a common understanding of the school's needs or strengths can be developed. It is important, therefore, that the report not be too polished or final-looking until reactions are incorporated. The school improvement team may serve this function initially, but you should also develop a plan for checking the initial results of the assessment widely with various groups within the school or district. The assessment report should reflect widespread understandings and the opinions of many.

Figure 6.
Imagining Success
(Defining Goals and Expectations)

- Before setting any goals, ask yourself two questions:
  1. What knowledge, attitude, or behavioral changes do I want to see achieved by whom (students, teachers, parents)?
  2. What do I want my classroom, school, or district to look like when implementation is complete?
- To clarify your answer to the second question, imagine you're hovering over your school in a helicopter. What you see is a close-to-ideal version of the new activity (for instance, use of microcomputers). Now ask yourself:
  1. What is going on in the classroom?
  2. How is the room organized?
  3. What materials and equipment are available or in use?
  4. Who is working with whom?
  5. What are teachers doing?
  6. What are the students doing?

When the assessment is completed, goals for the improvement effort should be set. (See Figure 6.) Goals should capture a description of what success would look like when the improvement effort is ended. What do you—and other important constituents in the district—want to see changed as a result of this effort? What will be acceptable to you as a measure of success? If you are initiating a revision of the science program, do you want to see improvement in students' scores on certain standardized tests or an increase in students selecting advanced electives? It is important that the goal be both specific and attainable in the time allotted.

A Conversation Between the Authors

Loucks-Horsley: *The assessment process described in this chapter sounds awfully time consuming and seems to contradict our belief in doing rather than assessing. What are some shortcuts to assessment that still result in a legitimate data base on which to act?*

Hergert: *In several projects where schools were committed to a two- or three-year process, we spent about three months on an assessment step quite similar to the one described here. Two things seemed to help us limit our data gathering. First, we called it "Problem Definition" rather than "Needs Assessment." We said we were trying to define more specifically what "hurt" and what improvements people wanted to see, rather than conduct research to document thoroughly the needs of the school. We cared more about action than accuracy.*

Second, we used the multiconstituent team as a major source of information. This information was not always in the form of verifiable data, but often it was perceptions, which we counted as data. We all agreed that if parents thought the school wasn't providing continuity between the grade levels, then that in itself was a "fact" that needed to be addressed. When we found that teachers also held the same belief, we accepted the need for continuity as a fact rather than spending time examining curriculum objectives.

The team also helped by collecting data. A teacher and a parent together developed a short questionnaire and surveyed all the parents who came to an Open House. Two reading specialists surveyed teachers, catching people in the lunch room and on breaks.

We found that by taking this informal, common-sense approach, we were able to get real, down-to-earth comments and criticisms—ones we had no question about how to interpret. Then we could get on to our tasks much sooner.

Loucks-Horsley: *I'm sure there are those who would say that because you didn't ask everybody in and around the school the same questions, your pool of information was unreliable. Furthermore, any action decisions you'd make would be real risky. How would you respond to that?*

Hergert: *I know you agree with me how important it is to actually do something to get people's real commitment and energy. But when a team acts on information, they don't set everything in stone. They agree among themselves—and then with the teachers who will be involved in implementation—to give something a good solid try. Then they can decide how it's working and make appropriate adjustments. Although I seem to be leaping ahead to evaluation now (and we'll talk more about this under Step 6), it's important to note here that decision making and implementing improvements are dynamic processes. When doing something (that is, implementation) starts, identifying the ideal solution doesn't end. By trying out the agreed-upon solution early (that is, not waiting a year or two until you're "sure," whatever that means), what is actually being done can come closer and closer to the ideal. Leaving room for discussion and reassessment brings the needs closer to being taken care of.*

Step 3: Identifying an Ideal Solution

The first part of the school improvement effort involves describing the current state of affairs and beginning to establish some goals for the improvement effort. It will be helpful to recognize and build on the good parts of the current program and staff. You will need to decide whether to replace a program or practice entirely, find another to supplement what is already in place, or educate staff to be more effective in some way. As you identify possible solutions, you will no doubt be considering full-fledged programs, instructional practices, materials, processes, and ideas. This is a complicated process, so we will discuss it in several sections:

- Identifying local resources and constraints
- Developing criteria for the solution
- Locating outside resources
- Applying criteria for solutions
- Making a decision
- Transforming a solution into a definable practice

The form and the content of the solution you choose are limited by the resources available. So we begin our discussion with these.

Identifying Local Resources and Constraints

As you examine the qualities of your present school program and staff, you should also examine the resources and constraints you have. First, is money available for improvement? How much and in what budget categories is it located? You may find that purchasing an entire textbook series is easier than freeing a teacher for training and planning. If you are involved in a major improvement effort sanctioned by the board, there may be a budget established and appropriated. If not, this is the time to begin identifying what resources you could access.

The information you obtained in the earlier relationship building should be helpful now. For example, you may have learned that the director of curriculum and instruction controls funds you need or that a particular principal wants to gain visibility in hopes of being promoted. You should know whom you will need to approach. Don't be discouraged if you fail to get what you want immediately. Often in the beginning you will be told that money is tight this year and won't be available. Then, as you make a compelling case and win over allies, suddenly money is there. Your task at this point is to "get the lay of the land." You should be able to tell if this is in fact a very bad year to ask for extra funds, if your project is a low or high priority for the school or district as a whole, and where there might be leeway.

Resources in a school system do not always equal money. Other kinds of resources may be even more important to you. Time is the one that comes most readily to mind. Time may already be set aside for teacher inservice; you may be able to get it allocated for your project. It may be possible to release a group of people from their regular responsibilities in order for them to participate in planning, development, or other project tasks. This may or may not cost money.

Time and money may represent constraints as well as resources. We have worked in school districts where the teachers were refusing to participate in extra activities as part of a job action. It was important to meet with the head of the teachers' association to determine exactly what that meant and how to involve people in the effort without interfering in this action. (We solved the problem by releasing teachers from classes and paying them for after-school meetings.) Other constraints may involve local political realities—certain issues may be controversial in a particular community, and the administration may have a particularly strong need to avoid controversy. Talking to a wide variety of people and keeping your ears open are ways of learning about both constraints and opportunities.

Developing Criteria for the Solution

Every need or problem has a number of possible solutions. Some will no doubt work in some situations, and others simply will not. Before you lose your perspective—your "view of the forest"—it is important to develop criteria for selecting a solution. The process of identifying criteria helps educators to decide what is important to them before seeing what is available. The criteria then provide a clear standard by which all resources, practices, and programs can be judged. In addition, using the criteria helps avoid being distracted by an attractive package or a high-powered speaker.

Before we continue, it is important to note what we think of as "solutions." Because your school improvement priorities may vary—from increased reading achievement to improved school climate or instructional leadership—solutions may come in different forms. They may be:

- Carefully defined, multicomponent programs with materials, instructional approaches, and teacher-support systems included;
- Instructional practices that change how teachers and students interact;
- Materials, equipment, or assessment instruments;
- Procedures for communication and/or cooperation among staff;
- A series of workshops focused on changing attitudes or skills; or
- A combination of any of the above.

Your search for solutions should not be constrained by the form they take, although, as we discuss at length in later sections, the better defined, more easily integrated into the classroom a solution is, the greater potential for real improvement.

What are useful criteria for selecting solutions? First, identify what elements are important to you. *Cost* of potential solutions will be among the earliest criteria to be identified. When considering cost, it is important to identify both start-up and ongoing expenses as well as categories of expenses. For example, will the solution involve new materials, teacher training, or new personnel? If training is involved, will the whole staff need to be trained or just a core group? How long is the training?

Less tangible, but often more significant selection criteria relate to the goals, philosophy, and norms of the district and the resources to be used. These criteria are often difficult to articulate but are essential to success. Some of these criteria include teaching style, instructional grouping patterns, types of materials, and student learning modes. Figure 7 is an excerpt of the Curriculum Analyzer, a tool that can be used to assess the importance of various criteria. It is important to identify the preferred criteria and to make certain that various groups in the school affected by the proposed change agree on them. It does not matter that everyone agrees that "individualization is important" if there are six different interpretations of what individualization means. If only the administrators have agreed on the criteria for selecting a new elementary science program, for example, the chances are slim that science teachers will eagerly implement it.

Figure 7.
Categories of Criteria for Solutions

PRIMARY TEACHING/LEARNING METHODS USED	Preferred	Alternative #1	Alternative #2
Lecture/Demonstration			
Memorization			
Programmed Instruction			
Laboratory/Practical Experience			
Discussion/Seminar			
Research/Synthesis			
Discovery/Inquiry			
Other (describe)			

Number of "Matches"		
Weighted Score (No. of matches times overall weight given this category)		

OVERALL WEIGHT GIVEN THIS CATEGORY: _____

Figure 7 (cont'd.)

TEACHER FUNCTION (Relation to Learner)	Preferred	Alternative #1	Alternative #2
Information Purveyor			
Diagnostician/Prescriber			
Contractor			
Resource Person			
Fellow Learner			
No Teaching Function			
Other (describe)			

Number of "Matches" _____

Weighted Score _____
(No. of matches
times overall
weight given
this category)

OVERALL WEIGHT GIVEN THIS CATEGORY: _____

STUDENT FUNCTION (Relation to Teacher)	Preferred	Alternative #1	Alternative #2
Listener/Follower			
Mutual Planner/Performer			
Primary Planner/Performer			
Fellow Learner			
Self-Instructor			
Other (describe)			

Number of "Matches" _____

Weighted Score _____
(No. of matches
times overall
weight given
this category)

OVERALL WEIGHT GIVEN THIS CATEGORY: _____

Figure 7 (cont'd.)

EVALUATION OF STUDENTS	Preferred	Alternative #1	Alternative #2
Evaluation Procedures Included			
Procedures Consistent with Objectives			
Procedures Tested by Developer			
Procedures Compatible with School's Grading Philosophy and Procedures			
Students' Success Evaluated by:			
Teacher			
Student			
Both			
Other (Standardized Tests, etc.)			

Number of "Matches" _____

Weighted Score _____
(No. of matches
times overall
weight given
this category)

OVERALL WEIGHT GIVEN THIS CATEGORY: _____

Figure 7 (cont'd.)

CLASSROOM STAFF	Preferred	Alternative #1	Alternative #2
Independent Teacher/Planner			
Independent Teacher/Team Planner			
Team Teacher/Team Planner			
Use of Teacher Aides/Paraprofessionals			
Resource Persons			
Series of Teachers			
No Teacher Organization Required (School can set up its own)			

Number of "Matches"

Weighted Score
(No. of matches
times overall
weight given
this category)

OVERALL WEIGHT GIVEN THIS CATEGORY: _____

Figure 7 (cont'd.)

MATERIALS	Preferred	Alternative #1	Alternative #2
Standard Texts and Workbooks			
Selected Readings			
Programmed Materials			
Laboratory Kits			
Games/Simulations			
A-V Materials			
Realia			
Other (describe)			

Number of ''Matches''

Weighted Score
(No. of matches
times overall
weight given
this category)

OVERALL WEIGHT GIVEN THIS CATEGORY: _____

Figure 7 (cont'd.)

EQUIPMENT REQUIRED	Preferred	Alternative #1	Alternative #2
Small Hardware:			
Television			
Film Projectors			
Slide Projectors			
Overhead Projectors			
Phonographs			
Audiotape Recorders			
Videotape Recorders			
Computer Consoles			
Other (describe)			
Large Hardware:			
Responder Systems			
Teaching Machines			
Other (describe)			
Specialized Equipment:			
Science			
Art			
Shop			
Cooking			
Sewing			
Physical Education			
Other (describe)			

	Alternative #1	Alternative #2
Number of "Matches"		
Weighted Score (No. of matches times overall weight given this category)		
Total Weighted Scores		

OVERALL WEIGHT GIVEN THIS CATEGORY: _____

Figure 7 is from "Curriculum Analyzer," *Designing Instructional Programs* (San Francisco: Far West Regional Laboratory, 1975).

Another important consideration in developing criteria is to evaluate how the solution will fit in with the rest of the district. Will the new program or practice involve a major or minor change? This is an important consideration for planning how much support will be needed.

The criteria developed at this point are not immutable. They are subject to change as discussion proceeds and as different resources, practices, and programs are examined. The school may decide on modifications in order to achieve other priorities. Criteria development is an evolutionary process that benefits from continued reconsideration.

Locating Outside Resources

Educators typically use a limited number of sources for locating solutions to their improvement needs. Commercial publishers and word of mouth are the two main sources for finding materials and programs. These sources are good ones and should not be ignored. Commercial publishers often have training programs to complement their instructional materials. Word of mouth can lead, not only to information about new ideas, but also to a sharing of resources with other educators. You can find out about people and programs through professional associations, conferences, journals, and newsletters. Moreover, you can search out educators or consultants who have actually had some experience with the practice, program, or materials.

However, even well-connected educators will find themselves limited if they use commercially published materials and word of mouth only. Billions of dollars of local, state, and federal monies have gone into developing a wide range of curricular materials and instructional programs. School staff should learn about these resources and use them in selecting their solutions.

Dissemination networks exist both nationally and in many states to allow schools to share different kinds of resources. In many states, departments of education employ a process to identify, validate (that is, to ascertain that its claims are credible), and disseminate (IVD) programs that were developed in schools within the state. The National Diffusion Network, supported by the U.S. Department of Education, makes successful improvement programs available through a facilitator office located in each state. (A list of these and other resources with contact information can be found in the appendix.)

School curriculums, instructional practices, and management tools have been developed on the basis of research and field testing at federally funded regional laboratories and research and development centers. In addition, there may be universities, private agencies, or other resource developers that should be explored.

Information centers exist in many parts of the country, both as independent agencies and as parts of intermediate service agencies, state departments of education, and so forth. Such centers have access to ERIC and other sources of information. (Several are listed in the appendix.) Although they do include some school-relevant programs and practices, they primarily house papers and articles that can provide background information or ideas to the school improvement team or other educators.

The important thing is to cast your net widely so that you have a broad array of resources—programs, practices, consultants, materials, ideas—to consider.

Applying Criteria for Solutions

You will need to collect information about the variety of solutions available in all their forms. In addition to descriptive materials, you should try to collect samples of what you will get if you select this solution. For example, a consultant should give you a proposal with a description of his or her operating philosophy and the kinds of services you will receive; a curriculum developer should provide the learning objectives, sample lessons, and a description of other materials needed to use this particular curriculum. Enough information and samples should be collected to enable you to assess how each resource fits your criteria and to compare one to another. Figure 8, on page 28, is an example of a form that could be used to assess several sample solutions.

You will need to develop a method for applying your criteria and for soliciting the opinions of others. You might consider weighting criteria, for example, so that the more important standards count more heavily. You will need a scoring system to use with the solutions selected for analysis. More than one person should judge each solution in order to provide a cross check or face validity to the analysis. Raters might be organized into teams of two or three or might consecutively rate solutions so that each is seen by several different people. This is another stage at which the school improvement team can be used effectively, and you might want to

Figure 8.
Mountain View Elementary School's
Evaluation of Consortium Reading Materials

Criteria	AIRS	PEGASUS/ PACE	WISCONSIN DESIGN		
1. Provides continuity for elementary reading programs through grade 6.					
2. Provides clear scope and sequence of skills.					
3. Provides teachers with ways to diagnose students' needs in learning to read, and strategies to teach to those needs.					
4. Encompasses many areas of reading program—word attack, comprehension, individual reading.					
5. Useful for students of a wide range of abilities.					
6. Encourages students to *read*—student as "do-er."					
7. Suits present staffing pattern without requiring new roles.					
8. Provides a useful record-keeping system to track student progress.					
9. Fits in with logistics of Mountain View schools (resource availability and sharing, class organization, and so forth).					
10. Flexible enough to be used by teachers with different approaches.					

General comments:

broaden review of resources to seek the opinion of everyone who is a potential user.

The form in Figure 8 was developed by a team, using the criteria they had worked hard to articulate, to help the faculty of an elementary school assess several programs. Program materials—descriptions and samples—were displayed in the library for teachers to examine in their free time. The simple form the team developed helped them to collect teachers' opinions and to focus on the identified criteria. Looking at the solutions at this point will probably mean looking at their "artifacts"—written descriptions, brochures, sample materials, guidebooks, and so forth. Very often, it is hard to get a clear sense from print materials. However, by using the criteria, many clearly inappropriate solutions can be eliminated. People can check on each other to make sure that eliminations are made for sound reasons and that information is complete.

For the solutions that remain after this initial elimination, you will probably identify questions that need answering. Perhaps additional materials are needed that provide more information. Perhaps a phone call could be made to the developer or representative, or an interview could be set up. Films and presentations about the solutions may be informative.

Gradually you will be narrowing choices by gathering more and better information. You will find that you get better at asking questions. The best test of a solution is to see it in action and to talk to users. Observations of a program or practice in use in other schools, or discussion with other educators who have worked with the consultant, will be especially helpful. Try to find classes where the practice has been used successfully for over a year. Keep an analytical mind: it is easy to be discouraged by teachers who are dissatisfied or to be converted by enthusiasts. Their reasons may not be yours; nevertheless, their experience and perceptions will be informative. Ask questions that will help you get the information you need.

At this stage, balance and objectivity are especially important. You and others will hear developers "pushing" their products and brushing aside any obstacles—or will hear about all the problems of a given program by implementers who were given inadequate support. Your task is to probe carefully and look objectively at the qualities of what you see and consider how it would work in your school or district.

Making a Decision

Eventually, the group must make its choice. If the process has been a careful and deliberate one, the choice may, by now, seem agonizingly long in coming. It is important to remember that care taken in making the decision will bear fruit in implementation.

Along the way, there should have been checks on how the decision will be made. Everyone needs a clear perception of their role. Are the people involved a decision-making or an advisory group? What is the role of the faculty at large? Will the superintendent make the final decision or abide by the group's choice?

The team leader must raise these issues periodically, must remind people of their agreements, and must develop strategies to ensure that everyone is informed and involved appropriately at each step.

How the decision will be made and who will make the decision are questions of equal importance. Will there be a vote with a plurality decision, or is consensus desired? A plurality decision that a substantial number of people oppose may impede successful implementation. It is important to reach a decision that is supported widely or, at least, is not actively opposed by a significant group.

When the decision is made, care should be taken to publicize it well. If the decision is made by staff, it may be helpful, or required, to make a presentation to the school board, depending on the size of the district, the importance of the program in the district, and political factors. Press coverage should also be considered; care should be taken to describe the chosen program carefully as well as to describe the process and reasons that led to its selection.

Transforming a Solution Into a Definable Practice

It is important now to consider the actual form of your selected solution. We begin here by sticking our necks out and calling on our research and experience to support us in saying: school improvement *cannot* happen unless something observably different occurs between teachers and students. Some may say that that argues for *all* school improvement efforts to involve a new classroom practice—one that improves the act of teaching and so the process of learning. In many cases we would agree. But we also believe that school improvement projects that target more general areas, such as school climate, curriculum renewal, and teacher expectations can be, and *should be*, thought of as attempts to change what happens between teachers and students. For example, improving school climate may mean promoting sharing between teachers and increasing teacher input into decisions about curriculum and instruction. These actions may increase the chances that teachers will use a greater number of approaches and activities that promote learning and fewer that inhibit it. Another example: curriculum renewal (updating and applying research on how students learn different kinds of material) must be viewed as more than just substituting one new set of materials for another. The way a teacher engages a student with content, the opportunities for approaching it in different ways, and the act of inquiring into an area and developing new knowledge—these require new behaviors on the part of teachers that should be part of renewing a curriculum.

The important questions to ask here are the following: What is going on in a classroom when our solution has been applied? What are teachers doing? What are students doing? How are they interacting?

For some solutions, these are easy questions to answer, particularly those that are programs or practices that have been developed somewhere else and used by a number of teachers in a number of schools. For materials and equipment that have been identified as a solution, this is less often the case. "What will teachers actually *do* with them?" is the question to be considered. (A microcomputer put in a classroom is a classic case in which this question is rarely asked early enough.) Research findings are another "solution" that are often difficult to define in terms of teacher behavior. "What do you mean, I have to increase my time on a task?" or "my expectations for students?" Those are two questions we often hear from teachers. Finally, a consultant—no matter how widely reputed or energizing—should be pushed to answer the same question: "When you have delivered your message, what should teachers and others be doing?"

The less defined your solution is, the more you take the role of its "developer." And we need to point out here that the more energy and resources you expend on development, the *higher the cost.* We want to discourage new development of programs or practices where others already exist to adopt or adapt. Research clearly points out that teachers can and do use practices developed by others willingly and faithfully when those practices are good ones (that is, when they can be described clearly and when they have evaluation data to support their effectiveness), are a good "fit" to the school or district (that is, they meet your selection criteria), and are introduced with the kinds of training and supplied with ongoing support that we describe in later chapters in the book (Crandall and Loucks, 1983). *Developing your own program can cost as much as 20 times as much as adopting an existing program.*

Whatever the form of the "solution" you have chosen, it is important to define it in terms of classroom practice. We have found that the development of a Practice Profile (Loucks and Crandall, 1982) helps to clarify and summarize program components and requirements. The Practice Profile gives everyone a clear, concise image of what a practice looks like and what is expected of them.

The Practice Profile has several parts. A Component Checklist identifies a manageable number of components (that is, Instructional Program, Materials, Instructor's Role) that describe the practice in use (Heck and others, 1981; Loucks and Crandall, 1982). What does someone do when using the practice? As an example, Figure 9 lists the components of a microcomputer-based writing program called QUILL.

In addition to a list of components, a Component Checklist "scales" each component, describing how it is used in the most ideal way, what way(s) is acceptable, and when the use (or lack of use) of a component is unacceptable. Figure 10 (p. 34) is an excerpt from the complete QUILL Component Checklist, providing more detail for several of the components. Note that descriptions of ideal use are to the left of the dashed line; acceptable uses are between dashed and solid lines; and unacceptable uses are to the right of solid lines.

The next part is Implementation Requirements, which describe training, facilities, personnel, equipment, and other resources needed to implement the practice. Figure 11 (p. 35) is a list of the implementation requirements for QUILL.

By defining the new practice and what is needed to implement it, you will help everyone in the district know what to expect and what to look for. The practice can be monitored and evaluated using the description, and needed modifications can be made.

After the program or practice is selected, local educators begin the process of implementing it. Now, the really hard part begins!

Figure 9.
Components of QUILL

QUILL Software
1. Use of all three programs: PLANNER, MAILBAG, LIBRARY.
2. Students use PLANNER for prewriting, compose first drafts for the LIBRARY, and revise their writing using WRITER'S ASSISTANT.
3. Teachers give QUILL assignments across the content areas.

Process Approach to Writing
4. Pre-writing activities precede actual composing.
5. Students write in different genres.
6. Students write to different audiences.
7. Revision includes both content and mechanics.
8. Teacher/student conferences are held.
9. Students work in pairs on QUILL assignments.
10. Students share their writing.

Classroom Management
11. QUILL is available for use by students every day for a significant amount of the day.
12. Each student uses QUILL at least one half hour per week.
13. All students in the class have the opportunity to use QUILL.

A Conversation Between the Authors

Hergert: *People talk a lot more now about promoting change in schools and a lot less about adopting or implementing innovations. I overheard a person criticizing a conference presentation on innovation as being "passé." Does that mean that all the work you've done on innovations—which we've imbedded in this book and this past chapter to a great degree—doesn't have anything to say for people interested in "promoting change"?*

Loucks-Horsley: *I certainly hope not. Perhaps this is my own special bias, but I believe that every time you're promoting change, you're talking about adopting an innovation. In several instances I've found this bias to come in handy.*

First, it keeps me from being criticized for encouraging change for change's sake. My opinion is that "if the thing ain't broke, don't fix it." One of the reasons that education is now in trouble is that in the 1960s and 70s we went around fixing a lot of things that weren't broken, often using untested panaceas that were far worse than what they replaced. So promoting change has a negative connotation for me—I want to know what is to be changed and how, and that requires, among other things, defining what I would call an "innovation" and then going about implementing it well.

Figure 10.
Excerpt from QUILL Component Checklist

Ideal	Acceptable	Unacceptable
Component 3: Integration With Other Content Areas		
Students frequently use QUILL for writing in content areas.	Students infrequently use QUILL for writing in content areas.	Teacher never uses QUILL for writing in content areas, but students write in content areas without QUILL. Students never write in content areas.
Component 5: Writing in Different Genres		
Teacher gives students QUILL writing assignments in several different genres.	Teacher gives students QUILL writing assignments in one or two genres.	Teacher does not use QUILL but: (a) students typically write in several different genres; (b) students only write in one or two genres.
Component 7: Nature of Student Revision		
Student revision reflects a balance between content and mechanics.	Student revision focuses only on content.	Student revision focuses only on mechanics. Students do not revise.
Component 13: Students Using QUILL		
All students in classroom use QUILL.	About half of the students use QUILL; these are (a) gifted or high-achieving students, (b) learning disabled or low-achieving students.	Fewer than half of the students use QUILL; these are (a) gifted or high-achieving students, (b) learning disabled or low-achieving students, (c) other special groups. No students use QUILL.

Figure 11.
Implementation Requirements for QUILL

Training
- Three days of released-time for training teachers prior to use
- One-day classroom coaching after use begins
- Follow-up sessions periodically during first year
- One-day extra training for local facilitator

Facilities
- No new facilities required

Personnel
- No new teaching personnel required
- Local facilitator must be assigned who has responsibility for trouble-shooting, follow-up sessions after training, and maintaining contact with trainers

Equipment
- Apple computer with two disc drives for each teacher (or shared between two teachers)
- Printer for each computer (or shared between two computers)

Materials
- QUILL software for each teacher
- QUILL Teacher's Guide for each teacher
- Blank discs
- Printer paper

Note: QUILL was developed by Bolt Beranek and Newman, Inc., and The NETWORK, Inc., under a contract with the U.S. Department of Education. QUILL software is available from DCH Publishing Company, and QUILL training is available from The NETWORK through a contract with the National Diffusion Network.

Many people view the phrase "adopting an innovation" as too neat, narrowly prescribed, and simplistic for today's schools. Some innovations do indeed fit that description.

But I prefer to define the word "innovation" quite broadly as any program, practice, process, or idea that requires new behaviors of its implementors. The correlates of effective schools constitute an innovation. Each correlate can be described as a set of behaviors that someone must demonstrate. What does someone do who is an "instructional leader"? What do teachers do who have "high expectations" for students? What classroom-management strategies do teachers use whose students exhibit high proportions of "time on task"? In my opinion the correlates of effective schools can be viewed as innovations to be implemented—not easily, simply, or neatly—but implemented, nonetheless.

Finally, some people believe that promoting change or school improvement can only be successful when teachers are supported to analyze their own teaching and to improve what needs improving. For me that too constitutes adopting an innovation. Whatever it is that individual teachers choose to do will require changing behaviors (unless they are kidding themselves or you). The actual innovation will vary from teacher to teacher, but making the change will be the same as implementing it.

I've taken to using the word "innovation" a lot less frequently than I used to, for the very reason that people are sometimes put off by it. But that doesn't mean I've stopped applying what I know about implementing innovations to the various changes today's educators propose and are actually making in schools.

Step 4: Preparing for Implementation

Now that your school improvement ideas are beginning to form a clear image, it's time to prepare to make them a reality. Preparing to implement the school improvement practice that you have selected involves at least seven activities:

- Creating awareness
- Selecting implementors
- Assessing current practice
- Setting expectations
- Assigning support roles
- Making logistical arrangements (for training, materials, facilities, personnel)
- Creating a timeline of activities and events

These activities have no particular sequence, but they do need to result in a clear, shared idea of what's to come—a map for "getting on with it." The more you and your team consider each of the areas listed above, the clearer your notion of how to proceed will become.

Creating Awareness

As we noted in earlier chapters, the best strategy for improving schools is to keep the important players aware of what you are

doing as you proceed. At each step, different people need to know
different things.

Now that you've chosen a practice, ideally with the input of
many others outside your planning team, it is time to give others
(teachers, administrators, parents, and so forth) the same image as
you have of the "what" and some indications of the "how."
Referring back to the CBAM, the questions being asked by those
outside the team (and many inside, as well), are self-oriented: What
is it? and How will it affect me? This means you should *not*
immediately plunge into extensive how-to-do-it training or spend
long sessions describing and illustrating the outcomes you expect
will occur for students. Short overview, descriptive sessions are
called for, conducted by a team member (or pair) who can talk about
what it will look like when in use (for example, teacher and student
roles, materials, timing). Sharing a component list such as that in
Figure 9 is a useful technique. The personal concerns are responded
to by describing the timeline and logistics: when training will occur,
when use will begin, and what the support structure is that will
back them up. (We'll say more about expectations such as these
later.) An opportunity to have questions answered should round out
a good overview session. Such sessions can be conducted for groups
of teachers, administrators, support people, and even for school
board members, to keep them informed of progress and begin early
to clarify some of the ways they will be needed to engage directly in
or provide support for the effort. Figure 12 describes some examples
of ways to create awareness of a new program.

Figure 12.
Vehicles for Creating Awareness

- In one large district implementing a revision of their elementary-
level science curriculum, a **slide-tape show** was developed to give
teachers, administrators, parents, and community members an idea of
what was new and why.
- In a school that had selected a new reading curriculum, an **open
house for parents** gave improvement team members an opportunity to
describe the new program and how it would be used.
- A school district adopting QUILL included an article in the
districtwide newsletter about a pilot teacher's success with it in the
previous year.
- In a school working to improve its math program, members of the
school improvement team held **briefings for individual staff members** to
answer their questions and discuss the new program.

Selecting Implementors

Early in your preparation, you will need to select the staff to implement the program. You must decide whether implementation will be voluntary or mandatory and whether to begin the program in all classes or pilot test it during the first year in a limited number of classes. In making this decision, you'll need to carefully weigh the pros and cons.

Voluntary implementation can result in a divided staff, at odds over the new program. It can also increase the problem of articulation from grade level to grade level, especially if the power of a program is in its use over several years. On the other hand, mandatory implementation may set the teaching staff at odds with the administration or the planning team. In part, this depends on the extent to which the process leading to selection of the particular program resulted in support strong enough to warrant involving all eligible teachers at once or whether a gradual involvement would be better.

If you decide to pilot test the program in a small number of classrooms, time limits should be set and criteria for effectiveness should be established. The selection of pilot teachers is an important issue. Volunteer teachers are likely to work hard but may not be representative of all teachers or grades for which the program is intended. A random assignment by grade will provide information about the program at all the appropriate grades but may involve teachers who are not interested in the program. A strategy in between these two is to go with teachers who volunteer and then fill in (by persuasion, negotiation, and so forth) where grade levels, expertise, and other factors are not represented so that a comprehensive pilot test results.

We suggest two things: go with the energy; that is, take advantage of enthusiastic teachers by letting them be involved when the program is initiated. Their enthusiasm will often be what it takes to get the majority, the "wait and seers," to risk trying it. Encourage opinion leaders—those teachers who others seem to respect, listen to, and go to for help—to be early users. And try to co-opt the negative, but good, teachers by giving them an early role and some responsibility. Many times this overcomes their negativity, and their strength as teachers contributes much to the program.

Assessing Current Practice

Consider this experience: A school has chosen to implement Project QUILL, the microcomputer-based writing program noted earlier that supplements a teacher's writing instruction. QUILL uses a microcomputer to help students plan, draft, and revise their writing, store it, and share it with others. As noted in Figure 9, three major dimensions of QUILL are a process approach to writing, use of the microcomputer, and classroom management for computer use.

When the QUILL planning team was ready to consider how to implement QUILL, they realized that teachers had a wide range of knowledge and skill with each of QUILL's components. The primary-level teachers had been using a process approach to writing for three years, but upper-grade teachers used a much more traditional approach; four of the teachers had been to computer in-services, few of the others had as much as sat down at a keyboard. The 3rd and 4th grade teachers were team teaching; they had mastered the art of using learning centers the previous year, so management of a computer in a learning center would be easy.

It is obvious that knowing what teachers are already doing with the components of QUILL—or any newly selected practice—is critical to planning an implementation. Grave mistakes can be made in the kinds of workshops conducted and the kinds of support given if assumptions are made that (1) teachers are all ignorant ("Our school hasn't entered the technological age."), (2) teachers are all doing something in particular ("We have a process-oriented writing program, so all the teachers are teaching that way."), or (3) teachers are all alike ("We're all starting in as blank slates.").

Common sense, as well as research, indicates the importance of assessing the current practice of each implementor with respect to the components of the new program. Using the Component Checklist discussed in the previous section can help. Once that is known, more relevant inservice and support can be planned.

Setting Expectations

Whether initial implementation is voluntary or mandatory, it is essential that appropriate administrators set expectations and standards for the effort. You may be an "appropriate administrator" if you can set standards and expect that they will be followed. If you are not, then you will need to convince appropriate administrators—

the principal, curriculum director, and so forth—to set the standards for the program.

Expectations must include:

- Giving the new program a fair trial, sticking with it for a specified amount of time.
- Refraining from making major adaptations, especially "watering it down," too early. In the trial period, fidelity to the program that was decided upon is an important expectation; only after becoming adept in the program and understanding how it works and can work better for students, should teachers make changes to suit their individual situation.
- Putting in the extra time needed to practice new skills, prepare new materials, and so forth.

In the very best situations, expectations are set by the school improvement team with the full backing of administrators and understanding and "buy in" of the staff that will be involved.

Making Logistical Arrangements

Often the implementation of new practices requires new sets of materials, new facilities (such as classrooms, labs, outdoor spaces), and new kinds of personnel (such as aides, bilingual teachers, lab technicians). These must be part of preparing for implementation. In addition, some new practices require rethinking and then rearranging the routines of both teachers and administrators. For example, sometimes practices call for more time to spend on a certain content area, more teacher planning time, more flexible classroom space, different teacher–student ratios. You need to identify all of the logistical arrangements and rearrangements that need to be made during the planning phase and then make sure that it becomes an ongoing task for the project's coordinator. (See Figure 13 on page 42 for some of the resources that may now be called for.)

Another item to arrange is training. First, consider the type and extent of training needed. From your assessment of current practice you can answer the question, "Do teachers need only orientation to new materials, or do they need extensive training in the program's new teaching strategies?" This will help you decide if you should plan a two-hour inservice or a series of one-day workshops.

Timing of training is also important and has financial implications. Depending on the time available and the amount of training needed, you may want to conduct a summer workshop, an after-school course during the school year, or a series of ongoing

Figure 13.
Possible Resources for Implementation

Money for:
—Trainers—initial *and* follow up
—Substitutes or teacher stipends for training
—Planning, meetings
—Materials
—Support personnel (coordinator, aides)
—Travel
—Equipment
—Evaluation

Time for:
—Information sharing
—Training—initial *and* follow up
—Support group meetings
—Administrative support, coordination
—Team meetings

seminars during the implementation period. Training during the school year usually involves the expense of substitutes. It may be difficult to find enough substitutes if you want to train a large number of teachers. Summer training may require teacher stipends that can be more costly than substitute pay. Training during the school year has the benefit of permitting trainees to quickly put their learnings to use.

The training should be conducted by people who are totally familiar with the new program, who are experienced trainers, and who understand the principles of adult learning (Crandall, 1983). The trainers could be the developers or representatives of the program, or they could be teachers or administrators who have worked with the new program in your or other districts. Before training begins, you should talk with the trainer to determine what will be offered, to share with the trainer the present skills of the teachers and their needs, and to identify needs that will not be covered during the training. For instance, the trainer may provide the teachers with extensive information about the program materials and teaching approaches but may not be able to help the teachers fit the program into their curriculum. Advance knowledge of this allows the planning group to compensate.

It is often worthwhile to conduct even initial training in increments: two or three sessions one or two months apart. This allows the teachers to learn a number of new strategies or curriculum units, try them, then come back for debriefing and additional training. Such a strategy keeps management concerns at a low level because teachers don't feel compelled to master everything at once, and they know they'll have an opportunity to share their problems and successes (Loucks and Pratt, 1979). At the same time that initial training is being scheduled, plans for follow-up training should be developed. By so doing, you will ensure that funds are available for follow-up training, and you will be providing an important source of support for teachers who are implementing the program—the promise of future expert help. Teachers are accustomed to seeing consultants come into their district, "lay on" a new way of doing things that disrupts all routine, and ride off into the sunset, never to be heard from again. This time, things will be different. The trainer, or another trainer with comparable expertise, will be scheduled to return, mid-year, to answer questions, help solve problems, and provide the next level of training. The return of a trainer can mean the difference between successful implementation and no implementation at all.

Assigning Support Roles

If we have learned one thing well, it is that teachers need ongoing support to successfully implement a new program and to integrate it into their teaching. This includes in-person assistance, material support, leadership, and moral support. To provide all of this, individuals other than teachers must be involved with the program.

Figure 14 (p. 44) lists a great many functions that need to be carried out in the implementation of a new program by the support structure you establish (Loucks-Horsley and Cox, 1984). You may want to designate a single person as the project coordinator—someone with some time and slack resources who is available to help teachers and "run interference" for them, especially at the beginning of the program. Or the functions may be divided up among several people, including especially enthusiastic and responsible teachers, principals, department chairs, central office staff members, or external consultants. In that case, someone needs to be designated to "orchestrate" all of the moving parts. Whether a coordinator with many roles, or charged with "orchestrating" others in their roles, this person is crucial to your project's success.

Regardless of how the support functions are divided, you need to take special note of several of them in preparing for

Figure 14.
Necessary Functions for School Improvement

Assessing needs, strengths, and resources
Assessing current practice
Setting clear goals, objectives, and expectations
Selecting or developing a new practice
Creating awareness
Assigning roles and responsibilities
Establishing commitment
Developing game plans
Allocating resources
Providing materials
Arranging training
Making schedule and organizational changes in school
Helping teachers plan implementation
Initial training
Problem solving and trouble-shooting
Providing follow-up training
Monitoring classrooms for use
Evaluating implementation outcomes
Evaluating ultimate outcomes
Training new or reassigned staff
Conducting follow-up and refresher sessions
Incorporating program into curriculum guidelines
Routinely purchasing new materials and supplies
Establishing a budget line item

From S. Loucks-Horsley and P. Cox, "It's All in the Doing: What Research Says About Implementation." Paper presented at the annual meeting of the American Educational Research Association, New Orleans, April 1984.

implementation. New programs often fall apart because someone decided that all teachers needed was a "hit and run" workshop to learn new skills and implementation behaviors. Now we know the importance of follow-up assistance that addresses the specific problems (often of a management nature) that teachers have after training. Demonstrations, coaching, problem-solving sessions, informal observations, and feedback—these are the kinds of support teachers need in that early period. (More about these in the next chapter.)

Specific, content-related help is important, but equally important is moral support. This can take the form of a casual word of encouragement. Or it can be formalized into a statement from the trainer and/or administrator that everyone knows change will not be easy, that it is okay to make mistakes, and that help will be there when it is needed. It is remarkable what a relief such words can be when teachers feel pressed by the everyday demands of teaching as well as having to master a new program. Yet, encouragement is not a technical skill that support and administrative staff learn to give in their preparation programs nor do they give it frequently enough.

Leadership is a form of support that is rarely placed in that category, but it is clearly part of any effective support system. The way leadership functions as support is in clarifying the goals and expectations and in monitoring progress toward them. Reminding people that the program is a priority and that everyone is expected to participate is a function that sometimes is forgotten after the press of initial implementation. Similarly, many people require a little "shove" to engage in something new, and this is a function that only people in leadership roles can play. Support systems that are built on mandates can be quite effective, but only if the practices they support make sense to teachers and result in student learning that is clearly visible to them. Then even the most reluctant teacher will be grateful for the initial push.

Creating a Timeline

Preparing for implementation of your school improvement project takes time, and it is sometimes easy to forget that the actual implementation takes time as well. Because we have an understanding of how change occurs, and the stages that people go through as they become familiar with and implement a new program or practice, we can create realistic timelines with important milestones.

A significant change takes three to five years from its initiation to the point at which it becomes truly incorporated into the ongoing life of a school and its classrooms. That gives some sense of the length of the timeline. One half to a full year can easily be spent in planning and preparing activities. The first year will focus on mastering the practice, perhaps by a limited number of teachers, and on establishing the support system needed to sustain it. The second and succeeding years will likely involve spreading the practice to other teachers, analysis of how things are working in early implementors' classrooms, and refinement. During that time also, the structures necessary for institutionalization (see the last chapter) are built to ensure continuation.

A Conversation Between the Authors

Loucks-Horsley: *When I talk to groups about school improvement, one of the most commonly asked questions is, "What do you do with resisters—the teachers who just won't buy into what's been decided on as a solution?" How do you respond to that?*

Hergert: *There are many different kinds of resisters, and they play different roles, depending on their concerns. Some resistance is both normal and healthy. If everyone goes along with all your proposals, never questioning or arguing, you can bet you are going to overlook something.*

It's important to find out about why people oppose the solution and to respond to misunderstandings or misinformation. Some people resist what they think is being proposed.

But let us assume that the process has included frequent information points, climate checks, and interpretations. In short, you've gone by the book and covered all the bases, and you still have resisters. Well, that's life! Some people resist anything new. Some people resist the specific innovation proposed because they have philosophical differences with it.

I repeat what we said in an earlier chapter—go with the energy. Use your supporters as implementers, keep lines of communication open with resisters, and try not to worry too much about them. If the solution works, people will come around later. The one caution I would add is to examine your group of supporters for significant gaps. If the supporters are the young "we'll try anything" teachers, try to persuade (or demand) a more stable and respected teacher to be one of the initial implementers. If you are trying to establish continuity between grade levels, try to ensure that every grade level is represented. Use your volunteers and also use persuasion to load your experimentation for success.

Loucks-Horsley: *For the most part, I would agree with you. If you'll pardon a gruesome analogy, dealing with resisters can be thought of like a medical triage à la MASH—one-third will get better without any attention, another third will come around with the right kind of attention, and the final third are beyond help! It's only the last group that I liken to resisters. Some of these folks will never move even with a great deal of attention, and they could consume many more resources than those who are more willing. Can you afford the time and energy to convince, cajole, bargain, coopt, and so forth? That's a very hard question, but one that must be asked (and answered).*

There's one more idea from my own research and experience that helps in dealing with resisters. Life is full of demands, and the status quo is usually much easier to live with than is change. So people will often opt out of opportunities if asked. School improvement leadership—both as a team and as individuals—needs to provide the extra shove that some people need to engage in your effort. Pressure, push—whatever the term—is a key ingredient for success. Time and again teachers have said to me that they would never have volunteered to implement a particular new practice—but are they ever glad they were given a shove (which often translates as "given no option"). Although I am not trying to paint a picture of the leader as a "thug," your role may sometimes call for making somebody else's decision for them—and then giving them all the necessary support to make their efforts successful. Well-designed and implemented school improvement projects have been found to win over even the hardest core resisters in the end.

Hergert: *The issue is to decide at what point to apply the pressure. If you engage in a trial period and need a limited number of people, pressuring a resister to be one of the first adopters may result in sabotage. The trial period especially should be loaded for success. After that, the program or practice can be made a requirement.*

Step 5: Implementing the Project

In a book on improving schools written by two people whose main interests and experiences have been focused on the implementation phase of change, it is remarkable how difficult it has been to write this particular chapter. There seem to be two reasons for this. First, almost everything that is done by and for people once implementation is underway can and should be planned for; thus, much of what might be in this chapter has already been discussed in the previous one. Second, there are often periods during implementation when the leader of the school improvement effort has little to do, especially compared to the frenzy of planning and initial training. Now, the effort is in the hands of the implementors. For you, this means sitting back, observing, and keeping "hands off" while the real users—the teachers and administrators most directly involved—put their "hands on."

There are, however, some key things to be done during implementation which, after all, is the stage at which an improvement effort either makes it to the classroom, or does not. What goes on in training and afterward is important, and here we offer more detailed suggestions than we were able to present in the last chapter. First, remember that concerns will be about *management*. The major question is, "How can I get this practice to work for me (so I can avoid going crazy)?" This question is expanded by the need for more detailed information about the practice and the continual need for the individual teacher to understand and integrate the demands of a new role.

How will you recognize these management concerns? You can expect rough going: poor coordination, lack of anticipation of what will come next, and classrooms that appear (and are) out of control. Few people are perfectly coordinated and can plan ahead successfully when they are first engaged in something significantly different. Accompanying these problems are feelings of frustration, annoyance, even anger at having to do all this different stuff as well as "carry on as usual."

This early disorder and dismay can, within a matter of months, evolve into a stable, satisfying routine, if teachers are given good training and ongoing support during implementation. We note this for three reasons. First, you and *everyone* involved (including teachers) should understand the process well enough to accept the rough part and not create unrealistic expectations of immediate mastery. Second, it is all the more reason to have a good, solid support system to deal with these very problems and minimize them. Finally, it now seems patently absurd to expect changes in student learning and be able to conduct an evaluation by the end of the first year.

As one implementing teacher told us, "You don't pull the flowers up every week to see how they're growing." If the going is rough for a good part of the year, there may be a time when kids may learn even less than with the previous practice. If the program you've chosen is a good one for your setting, you *should* expect increased learning, but *not* the first year. As we note in the "Review" chapter, ask if the practice is implemented and how it's going the first year; save an assessment of its impact on students until later.

But what kind of training and support will help to minimize management concerns and facilitate mastery of the chosen practice? In the next sections we suggest some answers.

Training

Initial training should respond to low-stage concerns: What is it and How do I do it? This means lots of information about the program's key features, approaches, and materials, given in detail so people know what they will be required to *do*. It also means hands-on experience with the materials, activities, and strategies so people have a chance to practice, to fail in a safe place, and to get help to do it better. The more experience people can get with what they will be doing in the classroom, the better.

Although engagement with the practice's "stuff" is important, there should also be time for teachers and other implementors to think about and plan for how they will fit the new practice into their ongoing work. What is the best timing, given certain scheduling requirements? Do materials need to be ordered, or can materials currently in use be incorporated? How? Giving teachers time to consider and work through these specific details alone and together can save them both time and headaches later.

When training is done in increments, it is important to know how participants have done in the interim periods. Have they mastered what they were trained to do? Have other concerns, problems, and issues emerged? Subsequent training sessions are best started with a sharing of the answers to these questions, either by someone who has taken the time to get them beforehand (see next chapter on monitoring) or on the spot in small groups with report-outs. How are people doing? What successes have they had? This way some informal networking of people can occur: problems with solutions, issues with ideas. Where have problems arisen? Sharing the discomfort of the early weeks makes people feel relieved that there are others in the same boat.

When training is spread out, people can be introduced to a limited number of components each time. For example, it's possible to train people first to use a certain piece of instructional software and incorporate it into current instruction. At the next training, other teaching strategies that make better use of the software than do current strategies can be focused on. Likewise, by using a Component Checklist, it is possible to introduce people to "acceptable" ways of using each component and then in later sessions to train them in more "ideal" uses.

As the first year goes on, some implementors will master the mechanics of the new practice and will begin experiencing impact concerns such as How am I doing? and How can I do better? Although there still may be some "basic training" to do, it is possible to offer several "tracks" at key points in training to meet the different concerns of all participants. For example, in training teachers to use a new elementary science curriculum, teachers were offered two sessions at the same time: problem-solving sessions on classroom management and a discussion on applying Piaget's ideas to teaching science. While teachers were given free choices, we noted that those who chose the former had been assessed to have significant management concerns, and those who chose the latter had fewer management concerns (Hall and Loucks, 1978).

Providing Ongoing Support

Several kinds of help are needed outside of training, including coaching, consultation, peer problem solving, and running interference. Although the content of training is dictated by the requirements of the new practice, the support that is needed throughout implementation is driven both by the practice and, even more, by the individual needs of the teachers.

Management by Wandering Around (MBWA) is a concept uncovered by Peters and Waterman (1983) in some of the best-run companies in the country. MBWA is one of the best tools for the school improvement leader to use during implementation. (See Figure 15.) One caution, however: be totally nonjudgmental and supportive. Teachers are feeling badly enough about being suddenly inept in their own classrooms. They must be reminded—and you must believe—that difficulties are perfectly normal, that they will soon master the new practice, and that help will be available. By wandering around, you want to accomplish two important things— to gather information about where the problems are and to provide encouragement and a pat on the back. Of course, after analyzing the problems, you will also want to assist where you can. Does the new equipment keep breaking? See that it's fixed or replaced. Is the 1st grade teacher experiencing a problem that the 3rd grade teacher has solved? Pair them up. Are five teachers having the same problem? Schedule a problem-solving session. By resolving, or at least addressing, little problems, you will be helping to keep the implementation on track and will be creating a positive climate.

Figure 15.
Some Things to Look For While Wandering Around

- Use or nonuse of new practices and materials
- Successful implementors
- Teachers having trouble, and what the trouble is
- Complaints and negative remarks, informal or voiced as jokes
- Logistical problems; for instance, paper shortages, storage problems, needs for new kinds of space or equipment
- Classroom management problems
- Teacher-developed techniques that work

If you think people will cover up their mistakes and fears in front of you, there are other ways to keep in touch with teachers during this period. Members of the team can divide responsibility for checking in with teachers, or you could ask one person from each group (k–3, 4–6, or English department, math department) to gather information within that particular group.

The concept of coaching, as introduced most recently by Bruce Joyce and his colleagues, involves guided practice by the teacher in the behaviors required by the new process. Coaching has a pedagogical as well as moral support function. When someone can observe a teacher's behavior and provide constructive feedback, teachers can avoid developing and maintaining bad habits. Mastering something incorrectly is a frustrating waste of time, whereas having guidance when they're first trying something new can help teachers answer the question, "Am I doing it right?"

Our experiences with coaching also reveal the psychological value of not having to struggle alone. Note that this reaction can only occur when the observer is *not* in an evaluative position and when the stage has been set such that everyone expects a rough beginning. Oftentimes coaching is provided in an actual helping role; for example, the observer may supervise one part of a class while the teacher tries his or her new skills with another part.

Another ongoing support role is running interference for new implementors. This means minimizing other requirements on teachers while they are struggling with the first few months of a new practice. A principal, for example, let teachers concentrate on introducing QUILL into their classrooms and told them he wasn't as concerned about having their reading and math lesson plans for a while. That same principal refused to let visitors come and observe (this included other teachers, schools, and districts) until his teachers felt comfortable in their classrooms. The result: a great sigh of relief from teachers and time to attend to using QUILL well.

What does all of this mean on a day-to-day basis? It means that the teachers can get the materials and personal help they need when they request them; that the support system is responsive to the needs of the implementors. It also means that people "show up" frequently in the classrooms or around the teachers' lounge to find out how things are going and whether help is needed; this support system is proactive as well. It means running interference for teachers, protecting them from administrators making new demands on their time. Finally, it means that people in leadership roles make public statements about the importance of the program and integrate it into what they think is important for the school: the goals, curriculum, staff evaluation, interactions with parents and community, and so forth. A good support system keeps teachers from "forgetting" to use a program. With it, they continue to improve use of the new program.

A Conversation Between the Authors

Hergert: *During the implementation period, it may be hard for the facilitator or leader to know what to do to be helpful. Teachers are busily implementing; they need concrete help with the details. The person who is managing the process, who played so central a role in the beginning, now is much less central and may think it is time to move on to new projects and interests.*

Implementation assistance is essential to the success of the project, but there's little glory in it! I remember teachers asking what my role was during this time period and not being sure how to answer. They valued the assistance of the program expert, not the process specialist (me!), as they struggled with implementing a new program.

Loucks-Horsley: *That experience brings up a very important point in the whole school improvement process. Perhaps it is best said that leadership is not leadership is not leadership. Different kinds of leadership and assistance are needed at different points in the process, and the person in the spotlight at one time will be backstage at another.*

What does this mean for who does what? First, it may be that people simply switch their upstage and backstage positions. Whereas the team leader spends relatively little time quietly monitoring progress during implementation, the program expert (be it teacher leader, district curriculum specialist, outside consultant) is much more visible working with teachers. Other team members may turn some of their attention to informing parents, school board, and other schools—something they had little time for earlier. Again, a dynamic set of roles and responsibilities.

Another thing this might mean is that it simply takes a different kind of leader to initiate an effort than it does to sustain and maintain one. Sometimes highly energetic, persuasive, cheerleading types fare poorly when their role changes to wandering around and finding out how things are going and, as we'll discuss at length in Step 7, being sure all the materials are reordered and new teachers trained. It may be that during implementation an orderly, systematic change of leadership is called for.

Hergert: *Right, but the key word is systematic. The leader may spend more or less time managing the project, but someone must make sure that the implementation is being attended to. That someone must also make sure to keep an eye on how the implementation is fitting, or disrupting, the organization as a whole.*

Step 6: Reviewing Progress and Problems

Once the flurry of initial implementation is over, it is time to ask "How are we doing?" Keeping a close eye on implementors and the implementation process is critical to catching problems while they are small, spotting areas where improvement is needed, and rewarding and reinforcing the people and events that have far exceeded expectations. In discussing this review process, we will cover three areas: (1) analyzing progress and perceptions, (2) evaluating outcomes, and (3) making refinements.

Analyzing Progress and Perceptions

Monitoring can use a mixture of formal and informal procedures. Certainly an important job of team members is to keep their eyes and ears open, creating opportunities to see things and be told things. This means purposely going out to schools, going into classrooms and teachers' lounges, and calling people for a catch-up chat. Filtering the comments and images through a concerns screen can help: Do the management concerns seem to still be there? Are personal concerns more or less apparent? Does anybody seem to care at all anymore? Sometimes labeling what we pick up by what kinds of concerns they represent helps team members share their impressions more easily.

Although informal procedures are important, you can be more objective and appear more accountable if you can describe progress and perceptions more formally. What are people actually doing that they weren't doing before? How are they feeling about their involvement, the new practice, their roles, and their impact? The first question—what people are actually doing—can be assessed in a number of ways. The most straightforward way is to use the same tool that helped define the practice in the first place and helped assess the current practice of implementors prior to training: the Component Checklist. For each of the practice's components, what is each implementor doing? This can be determined through a combination of interview and observation or it can be reported by the implementor or by someone in a key support role (project coordinator, teacher leader, principal). Although it is possible to come up with numerical values for the "extent of implementation" or "fidelity to the practice," the most useful way to analyze data from the checklists is to simply tally up how each component is being used by how many people. Eyeballing such a tally sheet gives immediate information about which components are still in the "not yet" stage, which are being varied the most, and which are going great guns and can be ignored temporarily. Figure 16 is an example of a report on how teachers in a school were implementing the 12 components of a science curriculum (Loucks and Melle, 1982).

Finding out what people are doing is one thing; determining how they feel about it is quite another. One tool for this brings us back again to concerns. A useful way to monitor concerns is through an Open-Ended Statement of Concerns (Newlove and Hall, 1976). Periodically, implementors are asked to write a response to: "When you think about _____, what are you concerned about? (Fill in the blank with the name of your program." Figure 17 (p. 60) is an example of such a statement, which clearly reflects management concerns. This rarely takes more than ten minutes, and can be done at a staff meeting, through teacher mailboxes, or at the beginning of follow-up sessions. Looking across a set of concerns statements can alert the team to the prevailing concerns, to danger signs should they exist, and to the range of things on teachers' minds. These statements can be formally scored or they can be a "quick and dirty" assessment. They can also be used to stimulate conversation or discussion in a meeting where at least a portion of the time is spent focusing on the school improvement project.

When there are more than 20 people involved in the program, or a more "rigorous" form of concerns assessment is needed, the

Figure 16.
Sample Building Summary Sheet

	Outside Intended Program	Getting A Good Start	Well on the Way	Best Practices Working	
	1 ------2------3------4------5				
1. Time is devoted to science	*** **	*	**	*	**
2. Science is taught according to R-1 Guide	*** ***	*** **			
3. Assessment of pupil learning	*** ***	*** **			
4. Integration of basic skills	*	***** ****	*		
5. The outdoor classroom is used as recommended		*** **	*** *	**	
6. Recommended materials, equipment, and media are available			*** **	*** *	**
7. Inservicing and financial arrangements have been made		*	*** **	*** **	
8. Long and short range planning			*** ***	***	**
9. Use of class time		**	**	****	**	*
10. Teacher-pupil interaction facilitates program		***	****	****		
11. Classroom environment facilitates program			***	***	***	**
12. Instruction is sequenced to facilitate the guided inquiry learning approach		**	**** *	****		

* = one teacher

School ___Winter Elementary___   Teacher ___All grade 3, 4, 5, 6, teachers___

Developed for the Jefferson County Public Schools Elementary Science Program. See Loucks and Melle, 1982.

Figure 17.
Example of an Open-Ended Statement of Concerns

Concerns Statement

When you think of the new math program, what are you concerned about? (Please be frank and answer in complete sentences.

The new math program is driving me crazy. I never know how many worksheets to have ready. The kids always seem to have their hands up for help. And I never spend less than 3 hours at home at night grading math sheets. Is it always like this?

Stages of Concern Questionnaire can provide a profile of concerns for each implementor (Hall and others, 1979). The profile indicates how intense concerns are at each stage. Figure 18 shows concerns profiles for two teachers: Teacher A is asking "What is it?" and "What does it mean for me?" and Teacher B clearly has needs in the management area. Profiles for groups, such as 4th grade teachers or pilot teachers, can be generated so that the data can be examined from a number of perspectives. Regular (for example, twice a year) use of the questionnaire can provide a clear picture of the progress of people's concerns about the program.

Evaluating Outcomes

We've sequenced this chapter as we have for a clear purpose: Assessing progress in implementation must always precede evaluating student outcomes. There are at least two reasons for this. First, since we know that early use of a significantly different practice can be quite uncoordinated and unpredictable, expecting student learning to improve in the first year is completely unrealistic. Do all the monitoring you want in Year One, but save the achievement measures. Second, once it becomes appropriate to use student outcome measures, it is critical to know what's going on

Figure 18.
Sample Concerns Profiles for Two Teachers

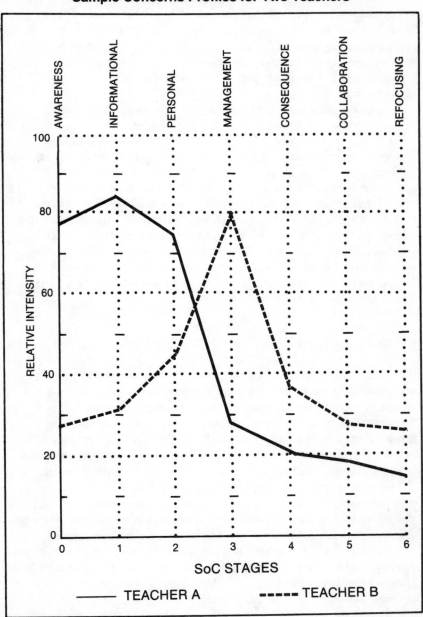

From Loucks and Melle, 1982.

that's causing whatever outcomes that result. Evaluations that result in a finding of "no significant differences" can have at least three explanations: the program is no good; the program wasn't being used by the implementors; and/or the control group (if there was one) was using as much of the practice as the implementors. It's all very confusing to interpret the results of such a summative evaluation if there are no implementation data. The message is: collect some.

Another note about outcomes. There is an endless list of possible outcomes for a school improvement effort. Look carefully at your list of goals before relying on only one outcome measure. Your outcomes may include a variety of student-growth measures: ability, performance, attitude, behavior. Or they may include teacher-growth measures in the same categories. Were you hoping for school-wide change in such areas as teacher collegiality, school climate, shared decision making? And what about the practice itself? Were you (or are you now) concerned with its spread to other teachers or other schools? Or with its continuation where it is right now? All of these are possible outcomes of a school improvement effort, and all are worth considering and then measuring as part of your indicators of success.

Making Refinements

Although reviewing a program after implementation is often for accountability purposes, the reason we encourage it is to find out where changes should or could be made. Again, we have an important purpose for putting this section well after planning and implementation. As we noted briefly in the last chapter, as well as in our discussion of setting expectations, there is an important issue around making changes in a new practice. Obviously, a practice that does not fit a situation well (for example, it was developed for different kinds of children, or it requires far more resources than are available) will most likely not work. But should a practice that has a great deal of appeal but does not fit your setting be changed substantially to make it fit? That is truly risky, since the practice was "proven" effective in its original form. It may be just as well to find another practice, or at least give the adapted one a stringent test before its use becomes widespread.

Our experience and our research tell us that changes need to be made in a practice with a great deal of care and concern (Huberman,

1983). What fits in one teacher's classroom may not fit in another's. And sometimes the definition of "fit" becomes closer to "preference." One teacher eliminates all the experimentation in a science program because it doesn't fit with his or her teaching style. Another gets rid of the "live critters" because having them requires so much extra work that it takes away from teaching time.

True refinements come when something's been tried faithfully, evaluated, and found inadequate. Changes that are made when people have management concerns are not being made with children in mind—just teachers. Changes made after a practice has been mastered and its effects on kids are assessed are much more apt to have positive consequences—for both kids and teachers.

It is up to the planning team to stay in tune with what teachers are doing and support well-founded refinements. Helping teachers "suspend disbelief" early on, and discuss and analyze desired changes, are tricky but highly worthwhile activities. Let them know that refinements are desirable and that there will be time and resources to make them.

In actuality, one of the most exciting times in a school improvement effort is when teachers have mastered a new practice and their concerns turn to its impact on children and how it can be refined. Teachers learn to look at their own teaching and that of others to gather data for change; they share ideas about what works and what doesn't; and they develop a norm of collegiality that benefits them far beyond the use of the particular practice they've implemented.

But all this can't happen by itself. Making refinements is one of the activities that we noted people must plan and budget for after implementation. Release time is often needed, as are resources for materials development and perhaps a return visit by the trainer. Providing opportunities for teachers to get together in which the agenda is theirs rarely occurs in schools. Making that happen and trusting the professionalism of teachers to bring good results is especially appropriate at this point in the process.

A Conversation Between the Authors

Hergert: *Evaluation of a project is important for many reasons. Teachers want to know if all this extra work accomplishes anything significant. Administrators and school board members need a reason to support the project and make it part of the life of the district. Parents want* *to know that the disruptions are worthwhile and that the school is getting better.*

Usually, everyone wants to see test scores improve. Yet, it is hard to get test-score changes as early as everyone wants them. What kind of information should planners seek at the end of the first year that would indicate positive progress?

Loucks-Horsley: *There is a great deal of information that can be collected at the end of the first year that can indicate progress. First, you can ask, "Is anything really different as a result of the project?" That is, "Have our efforts resulted in any changes?" Stick with implementation data to answer these questions. Describe what teachers and students are doing differently, what rearrangements (schedules, space) have been made, and so forth.*

By the end of the first year you should also be able to gather some perceptions of the project's influence on important outcomes. You can ask teachers, students, and parents about the project's benefits. Although achievement scores may not have leapt, you may get reports that students are clearly learning more, are less frustrated, like school better. Gathering informal interview data gives a good picture of these emerging results without prematurely pinning hopes on changes in test scores. A few good anecdotes about teacher and student successes often satisfy even administrator and school board thirsts for data.

I should note also that your task of reporting evaluation data is bigger than that—it's also necessary to educate your audience about what they should be expecting in terms of outcomes, and why what you are providing them at the end of the first year is important. This keeps you on the offensive, not having to defend why you aren't reporting test scores but saying why what you are reporting is of even greater value at this time.

Step 7:
Maintenance and
Institutionalization

You've analyzed your needs, found some better ways to do things, implemented new ideas, and refined them to best suit your students and your school. If the new program works well, you only have to sit back and congratulate one another, right? Wrong!

The last step in the process is to ensure that a successful practice is maintained in the school and becomes a regular part of the organization's norms and practices. Institutionalization does not just happen naturally. It takes planning and effort, often with people who, up to this point, have not been part of the effort. We will discuss three important tasks: (1) planning ongoing maintenance, (2) ensuring administrative supports, and (3) renewing staff commitment and skills.

Planning Ongoing Maintenance

Ideally, planning maintenance of your program should be thought about in the first stage of school improvement and again at each stage along the way. In reality, however, this rarely happens; when it does, many things can interfere. The school improvement effort may be funded as a project (by a business, foundation, or government sponsor) and ended when the funding stops. Or, the school system may budget this year for five people to be trained, only to find that next year (after a new school board is elected) it does not have money available to train the rest of the staff. Or, you may have assumed that if the program works in one school it will be mandated for all schools, only to find that the superintendent does not share that assumption.

Usually, one of two things happens after a trial period ends— either the whole program comes to a halt (with vestiges remaining among teachers who liked it) or the school district slides into full-scale adoption, without much thought given to that process. In either case, planning for ongoing maintenance is minimal and based on assumptions, often unarticulated and unchecked. With forethought, decisions can be made to ensure that a successful program becomes a part of the ongoing life of the district.

After reviewing implementation, assessing impact on students, and determining that the program is a success, a decision should be made about its continuation. It may be best for the superintendent or school board to make such a decision. They will need both information about the program's success and recommendations about how the program can be incorporated.

Often, there is an unspoken assumption that if the program works, everyone in the district should use it. This is not the only possible decision for maintaining a successful program. It may be that only certain designated schools will incorporate the program; it is even possible for the program to provide an alternative learning approach within a school to other approaches in use. First, a decision needs to be made about how the program will be maintained and what is needed for the program to become part of the school system. If the program is kept as an alternative, then one or more implementing teachers at each grade level will be needed as will a process for deciding how students are assigned to it. If the program is to spread to the whole district, you may need to plan another round of training.

Some thought will need to be given to training teachers who enter the program, often in ones and twos, through new hires and transfers. It is likely that there will not be a large enough group each year to warrant training. Therefore, some written materials may need to be developed, or an orientation and coaching system established. A new teacher could be paired with an experienced teacher for several months to learn from observation and discussion.

Figure 19 provides an example of a checklist used to remind school improvement teams about what they needed to do to "institutionalize" a program.

Figure 19.
QUILL Institutionalization Checklist

1. New staff receive training and orientation in the program.   _____

2. We have follow-up sessions for current staff to
   maintain the use of the program.   _____

3. The program is formally incorporated into curriculum plans.   _____

4. We have written guidelines for the use of the
   program's materials and methods.   _____

5. We purchase new materials and supplies in order
   to maintain the program's use.   _____

6. Our budget includes a separate line item
   for the program.   _____

Ensuring Administrative Support

During an initial period of implementation, normal
administrative procedures and lines of authority may have been
waived. For example, you may have been given authority to visit
classes or consult with implementing teachers, or the principal may
have given up staff meeting time for the program. Such
arrangements are usually temporary, and this is the time to think
about returning to normal.

Which administrators need to know about this program, and
what do they need to know in order to provide ongoing support? Of
course, you have maintained communication with various people in
authority throughout this process. But this is the time to "turn over
the reins" to others in the system. If the program will spread to
other buildings, those principals need information and assistance. If
there are support roles for central office people, they will need to be
negotiated.

This is the time when turf issues may arise and need to be
resolved. For example, the program may require extra resources that
cause others to lose resources. Or, the program may bump into
other programs (reading and remedial reading, for example) or into
new priorities ("reading was last year; *this* year we're emphasizing
math"). Your skills as a negotiator and organization member will be
needed here.

In order for a program to be maintained over time,
administrators must include the program's needs in their plans,
from evaluating staff to ordering materials. If the principal doesn't

notice whether or how well teachers are using the new practice, many teachers will discard it. Some programs require yearly expenditures for materials that must be included in the budget. As new initiatives are undertaken and move to the "front burner," your program must be one of the "givens" that are planned around.

In addition to individual bridge-building efforts, you will probably need a formal decision from the superintendent and/or the school board. You will use your evaluation data and present your case strongly and thoughtfully.

Renewing Staff Commitment and Skills

Beginning a new effort often results in a concentration of energy that raises morale and effort. Once the new effort is transformed into "the way we do things here," that energy can be lost. In addition to losing the burst of energy, old habits may reassert themselves and the practice itself may be lost.

Someone in the district should be given responsibility for periodically checking in with staff to make sure any wrinkles are ironed out and to identify new areas of growth. Often, a new practice will make staff more efficient in some area so that there is time to engage in more sophisticated activities in another area. Conversely, a new program may involve allocating more time for one subject and less for others.

In the ideal situation, your school improvement effort will never end. Instead, it will keep recycling itself into new spheres and new areas. The school should become a self-renewing system. Your goal may have started as a limited one to solve a particular problem, but ultimately your goal may expand to establishing a professional climate where everyone constantly strives for improvement. Such a school is not only better for students, but it is also an exciting and stimulating place for staff to work.

A Conversation Between the Authors

Loucks-Horsley: *Matt Miles (1983) points out a threat to institutionalization that everyone can relate to. A school improvement project has an advocate or champion who is responsible for much of its success, and lo and behold, by virtue of that very success, the advocate gets a juicy job offer and is soon gone, leaving the project to fend for itself. How can projects prevent this very common scenario from happening?*

Hergert: *There is no way to keep good people from leaving. I worked with a divided school district where the assistant superintendent was a great supporter of the project and could be counted on to step in at points of deadlock to resolve the conflicts. He left to become a superintendent just as implementation was beginning, and we had to figure out other conflict-resolution measures! I worked in another district for three years where, at the end of each year, our key "change agents" were RIFed (due to severe cutbacks, not persecution), and we started over again each year.*

A team really does help in these instances because there is already a base of support broader than a single individual can provide. Additionally, relationships have been built in the team, and sometimes a secondary leader steps forward.

The essential learnings are two. Don't rely too heavily on a single individual. *Keep lines of communication open with many people and make sure many people share ownership of the project. Second,* persevere even when the leader leaves. *If the effort* was *important to make, it is* still important. *You just have to keep going, filling in the gaps left until other people take over.*

You can and should encourage the person leaving to do whatever possible to put decisions in writing, to clarify who will have what authority, to provide some stability and support for the project at least for a while after he or she leaves.

Don't begrudge these people their success—wish them well! Usually, they have contributed to the progress achieved thus far; it's up to you to ensure that progress isn't lost. They will probably spread seeds of school improvement where they go next and will become part of your network of colleagues and supporters. Who knows? You may be next!

Appendix:
Resources for School
Improvement

The purpose of this appendix is to suggest some resources that may be useful as school improvement projects are designed, implemented, and maintained. Millions of dollars have been spent establishing mechanisms for schools to share successes, and to make readily available the abundant knowledge about what works. Here we include contact information for three such mechanisms:

1. *ERIC and ERIC Search Services:* the tremendous information base that, when used wisely and creatively, can provide information, ideas, products, and programs.

2. *The National Diffusion Network:* a federal program that supports the transfer of effective educational programs from schools that developed them to schools that choose to implement them.

3. *Regional Service Organizations/Laboratories:* organizations that exist around the country to bring schools a wide range of research and development-based products, programs, and services.

Educational Resources Information Center (ERIC)

In several states, the state department of education, regional service centers, county offices of education and other intermediate units, and/or school districts may provide information services to practicing educators. In addition, many college and university libraries offer search services; however, there is usually a charge. If you do not know the location of an organization providing information services, try checking with someone in your central office or with a contact at one of the organizations listed above.

The ERIC Processing and Reference Facility has compiled directories of ERIC search services and ERIC microfiche collections; the entries in both are organized by state, and the search service directory also indicates the client groups served by each search service. Information services that specialize in providing information for practicing educators tend to tailor their offerings to the needs of educators. We recommend trying them first.

The ERIC Processing and Reference Facility can tell you the location of information services in your locality, and send you the ERIC directories. Write or call:

ERIC Processing and Reference Facility
ORI, Inc.
Information Systems Division
4833 Rugby Avenue, Suite 301
Bethesda, MD 20814
Telephone: 301/656-9723

If it turns out that there is no available service in your state and you are considering paying for a search, we recommend contacting the SMERC Information Center in San Mateo, California. The staff at SMERC offers a variety of services at reasonable prices; they specialize in serving practicing educators, including SEA, intermediate unit, district, and school personnel alike. SMERC can also arrange contracts with your district or intermediate unit that cover a variety of services, such as online searches. If you belong to an organization that is engaged in school improvement efforts, such an arrangement could be a very good use of a relatively small amount of money. Write or call:

Sara Lake, Information Dissemination Specialist
SMERC Information Center
333 Main Street
Redwood City, CA 94063
Telephone: 415/363-5488

ERIC Network Components

There are currently 16 ERIC Clearinghouses, each responsible for a major area of the field of education. Clearinghouses acquire, select, catalog, abstract, and index the documents announced in *Resources in Education* (RIE). They also prepare interpretive summaries and annotated bibliographies dealing with high interest topics based on the documents analyzed for RIE, which are also announced in RIE.

ERIC Clearinghouses:

ADULT, CAREER, AND VOCATIONAL EDUCATION (CE)
Ohio State University
National Center for Research in Vocational Education
1960 Kenny Road
Columbus, OH 43210
Telephone: 614/486-3655

COUNSELING AND PERSONNEL
SERVICES (CG)
University of Michigan
School of Education Building, Room 2108
East University & South University Sts.
Ann Arbor, MI 48109
Telephone: 313/764-9492

EDUCATIONAL MANAGEMENT (EA)
University of Oregon
1787 Agate Street
Eugene, OR 97403
Telephone: 503/686-5043

ELEMENTARY AND EARLY
CHILDHOOD EDUCATION (PS)
University of Illinois
College of Education
805 West Pennsylvania Avenue
Urbana, IL 68101
Telephone: 217/333-1386

HANDICAPPED AND GIFTED
CHILDREN (EC)
Council for Exceptional Children
1920 Association Drive
Reston, VA 22091
Telephone: 703/620-3660

HIGHER EDUCATION (HE)
George Washington University
One Dupont Circle, N.W., Suite 630
Washington, DC 20036
Telephone: 202/296-2597

INFORMATION RESOURCES (IR)
Syracuse University
School of Education
Huntington Hall, Room 030
Syracuse, NY 13210
Telephone: 315/423-3640

JUNIOR COLLEGES (JC)
University of California at Los Angeles
Mathematical Sciences Building, Room
8118
405 Hilgard Avenue
Los Angeles, CA 90024
Telephone: 213/825-3931

LANGUAGES AND LINGUISTICS (FL)
Center for Applied Linguistics
3520 Prospect Street, N.W.
Washington, DC 20007
Telephone: 202/298-9292

READING AND COMMUNICATION
SKILLS (CS)
National Council of Teachers of English
1111 Kenyon Road
Urbana, IL 61801
Telephone: 217/328-3870

RURAL EDUCATION AND SMALL
SCHOOLS (RC)
New Mexico State University
Box 3 AP
Las Cruces, NM 88003
Telephone: 505/646-2623

SCIENCE, MATHEMATICS, AND
ENVIRONMENTAL
EDUCATION (SE)
Ohio State University
1200 Chambers Road, Third Floor
Columbus, OH 43212
Telephone: 614/422-6717

SOCIAL STUDIES/SOCIAL SCIENCE
EDUCATION (SO)
Social Science Education Consortium, Inc.
855 Broadway
Boulder, CO 80302
Telephone: 303/492-8434

TEACHER EDUCATION (SP)
American Association of Colleges for
Teacher Education
One Dupont Circle, N.W., Suite 610
Washington, DC 20036
Telephone: 202/293-2450

TESTS, MEASUREMENT, AND
EVALUATION (TM)
Educational Testing Service
Princeton, NJ 08541
Telephone: 609/734-5176

URBAN EDUCATION (UD)
Columbia University
Teachers College
Box 40
525 West 120th Street
New York, NY 10027
Telephone: 212/678-3437

SPONSOR:
EDUCATIONAL RESOURCES
INFORMATION CENTER
(Central ERIC)
National Institute of Education
Washington, DC 20208
Telephone: 202/254-7934

CENTRALIZED DATABASE
MANAGEMENT:
ERIC PROCESSING & REFERENCE
FACILITY
ORI, Inc., Information Systems Division
4833 Rugby Avenue, Suite 301
Bethesda, MD 20814
Telephone: 301/656-9723

DOCUMENT DELIVERY:
ERIC DOCUMENT REPRODUCTION
SERVICE

Computer Microfilm International Corp.
P.O. Box 190
Arlington, VA 22210
Telephone: 703/823-0500

COMMERCIAL PUBLISHING:
The ORYX PRESS
2214 North Central Avenue at Encanto
Phoenix, AZ 85004
Telephone: 602/254-6156

National Diffusion Network Facilitators

To help public and private schools and districts identify suitable National Diffusion Network (NDN) programs, the National Diffusion Network Division, federal sponsor of the NDN, supports facilitator projects in every state, the District of Columbia, the Virgin Islands, and Puerto Rico.

Facilitators work with schools and institutions to define their problems, determine which NDN programs hold promise for solving those problems, and help with formal adoption of NDN programs. Facilitators can supply additional information on all of the programs described in the book called *Educational Programs That Work,* and arrange for demonstrations. When a school or institution decides to adopt an NDN program, facilitators can make arrangements for training. Many facilitators also provide follow-up assistance and perform or oversee monitoring and evaluation of adopter sites.

NDN facilitators are based in local school districts, intermediate service agencies, state education agencies, and private nonprofit organizations. The funds that facilitators can draw on vary from state to state, as do their funding policies. In some states, schools and districts that adopt NDN programs can be reimbursed by the facilitator for such start-up costs as instructional materials and teacher training. In other states, the costs of travel to awareness conferences or demonstration sites can be covered by the facilitator. We encourage readers to telephone or visit their NDN facilitators to learn what services are available.

ALABAMA
R. Meade Guy
Facilitator Project
AL Information & Development Sys.
(AIDS)
Alabama Department of Education
Room 607, State Office Building
Montgomery, AL 36130
205/261-5065

ALASKA
Gladys Foris
Alaska State Facilitator Project
Alaska Department of Education
Pouch F, State Office Building
Juneau, AK 99811
907/465-2841

ARIZONA
L. Leon Webb
Arizona State Facilitator
Educational Diffusion Systems, Inc.
161 East First Street
Mesa, AZ 85201
602/969-4880

ARKANSAS
B.J. Confer
Arkansas State Facilitator
Arkansas Department of Education
Arch Ford Education Building
State Capitol Mall
Little Rock, AR
501/371-5038

CALIFORNIA
Jane E. Zinner
California State Facilitator Project
1575 Old Bayshore Highway
Burlingame, CA 94010
415/692-4300

COLORADO
Charles D. Beck, Jr.
Colorado State Facilitator Project
Northern Colorado Educational Board of
   Cooperative Services
830 South Lincoln
Longmont, CO 80501
303/772-4420 or 442-2197

CONNECTICUT
Sally Harris
Connecticut Facilitator Project
Area Cooperative Educational Service
295 Mill Road
North Haven, CT 06473
203/234-0130

DELAWARE
Walter Orr
State Facilitator Project
Department of Public Instruction
John G. Townsend Building
Dover, DE 19901
302/736-4583

DISTRICT OF COLUMBIA
Susan Williams
District Facilitator Project
Eaton School
34th and Lowell Streets, N.W.
Washington, DC 20037
202/282-0056

FLORIDA
Ralph Vedros
State Facilitator for the Dept. of Ed.
Division of Public Schools
Knott Building
Tallahassee, FL 32301
904/487-1078

GEORGIA
India Lynn King
Georgia State Facilitator
226 Fain Hall
University of Georgia
Athens, GA 30602
404/542-3332

HAWAII
Kathleen Steffen or Richard Port
Hawaii Educational Dissemination
   Diffusion System (HEDDS)

Office of Instructional Services
595 Pepeekeo Street, Building H
Honolulu, HI 96825
808/396-6356

IDAHO
Ted L. Lindley
State Facilitator Center
Idaho State Department of Education
Len B. Jordan Office Building
650 West State Street
Boise, ID 83720
208/334-2189

ILLINOIS
Shirley Menendez
Project Director
Statewide Facilitator Project
1105 East Fifth Street
Metropolis, IL 62960
618/524-2664

INDIANA
Ted Newell
Project Director
Indiana Facilitator Center
Logansport Community School Corp.
2829 George Street
Logansport, IN 46947
219/722-1754

IOWA
David C. Lindstrom
State Facilitator
Department of Public Instruction
Grimes State Office Building
Des Moines, IA 50319
515/281-3111

KANSAS
James H. Connett
Kansas State Facilitator Project
Director, KEDDS/LINK
1847 North Chautauqua
Wichita, KS 67214
316/685-0271

KENTUCKY
John C. Padgett
Project Director
Department of Education
Capitol Plaza Tower Office Building
Room 1700
Frankfort, KY 40601
502/564-4394

LOUISIANA
Charles Jarreau
Facilitator Project Director
State Department of Education

ESEA Title IV Bureau Office
P.O. Box 44064
Baton Rouge, LA 70804
504/342-3375

MAINE
Robert Shafto or Catherine Harding
Maine Facilitator Center
P.O. Box 620
Auburn, ME 04345
207/783-0833

MARYLAND
Raymond Hartjen
Project Director
P.O. Box 265
Simms Landing Road
Port Tobacco, MD 20677
301/934-2992

MASSACHUSETTS
Leslie Hergert or Denise Blumenthal
The NETWORK, Inc.
290 South Main Street
Andover, MA 01810
617/470-1080

MICHIGAN
Patricia Slocum
Michigan State Facilitator
Michigan Department of Education
Box 30008
Lansing, MI 48909
517/373-1806

MINNESOTA
Diane Lassman or Carol Johnson
150 Pillsbury Avenue
Pattee Hall
University of Minnesota
Minneapolis, MN 55455
612/376-5297

MISSISSIPPI
George Dukes
Mississippi Facilitator Project
Mississippi School Board Association
P.O. Box 203
Clinton, MS 39056
601/924-2001

MISSOURI
Jolene Schulz
Project Director
Columbia Public School System
310 North Providence Road
Columbia, MO 65201
314/449-8622

MONTANA
Pat Feely

State Facilitator Project
Office of Public Instruction
State Capitol
Helena, MT 59601
406/449-3082

NEBRASKA
Mary Lou Palmer
State Facilitator Project
Nebraska Department of Education
301 Centennial Mall
P.O. Box 94987
Lincoln, NE 68509
402/471-2452

NEVADA
Victor M. Hyden
State Facilitator
Nevada Department of Education
400 West King Street, Capitol Complex
Carson City, NV 89710
702/885-3136

NEW HAMPSHIRE
Jared Shady
New Hampshire Facilitator Project
RFD 3, Box 26A
Loraco Plaza
Concord, NH 03301
603/224-9461

NEW JERSEY
Katherine Wallin
Educational Information & Resource
   Center
NJ State Facilitator Project
Box 29
Sewell, NJ 08080
609/228-6000

NEW MEXICO
Amy L. Watkins or Susan Carter
New Mexico State Facilitators
Department of Educational Foundations
University of New Mexico
College of Education
Onate Hall, Room 223
Albuquerque, NM 87131
505/277-5204

NEW YORK
Samuel Corsi, Jr.
State Facilitator
New York Education Department
Room 860
Albany, NY 12234
518/474-1280

NORTH CAROLINA
Grace Drain

Project Director
Division of Personal Relations
Department of Public Instruction
Education Building
Raleigh, NC 27611
919/733-9230

NORTH DAKOTA
Pat Herbal
State Facilitator
Department of Public Instruction
State Capitol
Bismark, ND 58505
701/224-2281

OHIO
C. William Phillips
Ohio Facilitation Center
The Ohio Department of Education
Division of Inservice Education
65 South Front Street, Room 416
Columbus, OH 43215
614/466-2979

OKLAHOMA
Kenneth Smith
Statewide Facilitator
Edmond Public Schools
215 North Boulevard
Edmond, OK 73034
405/341-3457 or -9534

OREGON
Ralph Nelson
Columbia Education Center
11325 S.E. Lexington
Portland, OR 97266
503/760-2346

PENNSYLVANIA
Richard Brickley
Facilitator Project, R.I.S.E.
725 Caley Road
King of Prussia, PA 19406
215/265-6056

RHODE ISLAND
Faith Fogle-Donmoyer
Rhode Island State Facilitator Project
Rhode Island Department of Education
22 Hayes Street, Roger Williams Bldg.
Providence, RI 02908
410/277-2617

SOUTH CAROLINA
Ronald Mickler
State Facilitator
South Carolina Department of Education
1429 Senate Street
Columbia, SC 29201
803/758-3526

SOUTH DAKOTA
Maxine Schochenmaier
State Facilitator
Division of Elementary and Secondary
   Education
Richard F. Kneip Building
Pierre, SD 57501
605/772-4774

TENNESSEE
Martin McConnell or Charles M. Achilles
Project Directors
College of Education/Capitol BERS
2046 Terrace Avenue
University of Tennessee
Knoxville, TN 37916
615/974-4165 or -2272

TEXAS
Walter Rambo
Texas State Facilitator
Texas Education Agency
201 East 11th Street
Austin, TX 78701
512/475-6838

UTAH
Kenneth P. Lindsay
Utah State Facilitator Project
Utah State Office of Education
250 East 500 South
Salt Lake City, UT 84111
801/533-5061

VERMONT
Lynn E. Baker
Trinity College
Colchester Avenue
Burlington, VT 05401
802/658-0337

VIRGINIA
Andrew M. Lebby
The Knowledge Group
905 Portner Place
Alexandria, VA 22314
703/683-3138

WASHINGTON
Keith Wright or Bill Guise
Washington State Facilitators
15675 Ambaum Boulevard, S.W.
Seattle, WA 98166
206/433-2453

WEST VIRGINIA
Dave Purdy
W.V. State Facilitator
Building #6, Room B-252
State Department of Education

Charleston, WV 25305
304/348-2700

WISCONSIN
Thomas Diener
State Facilitator
Department of Public Instruction
Instructional Services Division
125 South Webster
P.O. Box 7841
Madison, WI 53707
608/266-3560

WYOMING
Jack Prince
State Facilitator
Wyoming Innovation Network System
State Department of Education
Hathaway Building, Room 236

Cheyenne, WY 82002
307/777-6252

PUERTO RICO
Maria Agosta
Puerto Rico State Facilitator
Center for Dissemination, 5th Floor
Department of Education
P.O. Box 759
Hato Rey, PR 00919
809/759-8240

VIRGIN ISLANDS
Phyllis Betz
Virgin Islands State Facilitator
Virgin Islands Department of Education
P.O. Box 6640
St. Thomas, VI 00801
809/774-0807

Regional Service Organizations/Laboratories

The Council for Educational Development and Research (CEDaR) is a Washington-based association concerned about educational improvement. The following organizations, which belong to CEDaR, are mostly federally funded regional educational laboratories. The NETWORK, Inc., is an independent educational service organization serving the Northeast.

APPALACHIA EDUCATIONAL
  LABORATORY
P.O. Box 1348
Charleston, WV 25325
304/347-0400
States Served: Alabama, Kentucky, Ohio,
  Tennessee, Virginia, West Virginia

FAR WEST LABORATORY FOR
  EDUCATIONAL RESEARCH AND
  DEVELOPMENT
1855 Folsom Street
San Francisco, CA 94103
415/565-3000
States Served: Northern California,
  Nevada (except Clark County), Utah

MID-CONTINENT REGIONAL
  EDUCATIONAL LABORATORY
2600 South Parker Road
Building 5, Suite 353
Aurora, CO 80014
303/337-0990
States Served: Colorado, Kansas, Missouri,

Nebraska, North Dakota, South Dakota,
  Wyoming

THE NETWORK, INC.
290 South Main Street
Andover, MA 01810
617/470-1080
States Served: Maine, New Hampshire,
  Rhode Island, Vermont, Connecticut,
  Massachusetts, New York

NORTHWEST REGIONAL
  EDUCATIONAL LABORATORY
300 S.W. Sixth Avenue
Portland, OR 97204
503/248-6800
States Served: Alaska, Hawaii, Idaho,
  Montana, Oregon, Washington

RESEARCH FOR BETTER SCHOOLS
444 North Third Street
Philadelphia, PA 19123
215/574-9300
States Served: New Jersey, Maryland,
  Pennsylvania, Delaware

SWRL EDUCATIONAL RESEARCH AND
   DEVELOPMENT
4665 Lampson Avenue
Los Alamitos, CA 90720
213/598-7661
States Served: Southern California,
   Nevada (Clark County), Arizona

SOUTHWEST EDUCATIONAL
   DEVELOPMENT LABORATORY
211 East Seventh Street
Austin, TX 78701
512/476-6861
States Served: Texas, Arkansas, New
   Mexico, Oklahoma, Louisiana,
   Mississippi

References

Clark, D.; McKibbin, S.; and Malkas, M., eds. *Alternative Perspectives for Viewing Educational Organizations.* San Francisco: Far West Laboratory, 1981.

Crandall, D.P. "The Teacher's Role in School Improvement." *Educational Leadership* 41 (November 1983): 6–9.

Crandall, D.P., and associates. *People, Policies, and Practices: Examining the Chain of School Improvement.* Vol. I–X. Andover, Mass.: The NETWORK, Inc., 1982.

Ford, J.J., III, and Hergert, L.F. *Linking Agent's Tool Kit.* Andover, Mass.: The NETWORK, Inc., 1979.

Hall, G.E.; George, A.A.; and Rutherford, W.L. "Measuring Stages of Concern About the Innovation: A Manual for Use of the SoC Questionnaire." Austin: Research and Development Center for Teacher Education, The University of Texas, 1979.

Hall, G.E., and Loucks, S.F. "Teacher Concerns as a Basis for Facilitating and Personalizing Staff Development." *Teachers College Record* 80, 1 (1978): 36–53.

Heck, S.; Stiegelbauer, S.M.; Hall, G.E.; and Loucks, S.F. "Measuring Innovation Configurations: Procedures and Applications." Austin: Research and Development Center for Teacher Education, The University of Texas, 1981.

Huberman, A.M. "School Improvement Strategies That Work." *Educational Leadership* 41 (November 1983): 23–27.

Loucks-Horsley, S., and Cox, P.L. "It's All In The Doing: What Recent Research Says About Implementation." Paper presented at the annual meeting of the American Educational Research Association, New Orleans, 1984.

Loucks, S.F., ed. "Ensuring Success: Good News From a Study of School Improvement." *Educational Leadership* 41 (November 1983): 3–32.

Loucks, S.F. "At Last: Some Good News From a Study of School Improvement." *Educational Leadership* 41 (November 1983): 4–5.

Loucks, S.F., and Crandall, D.P. "The Practice Profile: An All-Purpose Tool for Program Communication, Staff Development, Evaluation, and Implementation." Andover, Mass.: The NETWORK, Inc., 1982.

Loucks, S.F., and Hall, G.E. "Implementing Innovations in Schools: A Concerns-Based Approach." Austin: Research and Development Center for Teacher Education, The University of Texas, 1979.

Loucks, S.F., and Melle, M. "Evaluation of Staff Development: How Do You Know It Took?" *Journal of Staff Development* 3, 1 (1982): 102–117.

Loucks, S.F., and Pratt, H. "A Concerns-Based Approach to Curriculum Change." *Educational Leadership* 37 (December 1979): 212–215.

Louis, K.S., and Rosenblum, S. *Linking R&D with Schools: A Program and Its Implications for Dissemination and School Improvement Policy.* Cambridge, Mass.: Abt Associates, 1981.

Miles, M.B. "Unraveling the Mystery of Institutionalization." *Educational Leadership* 41 (November 1983): 14–19.

Newlove, B.W., and Hall, G.E. "A Manual for Assessing Open-Ended Statements of Concern About an Innovation." Austin: Research and Development Center for Teacher Education, The University of Texas, 1976.

Peters, T.J., and Waterman, R.H., Jr. *In Search of Excellence.* New York: Harper and Row, 1982.